Creating a Learning and Development Strategy

The HR Business Partner's Guide to Developing People

Second edition

D0231059

Andrew Mayo is Professor of Human Capital Management at Middlesex University Business School and Director of Mayo Learning International Ltd, a consultancy specialising in developing human capital. He is also Fellow and Programme Director for the centre of Management Development at London Business School. He spent 28 years in international organisations before taking up his portfolio career. He is married with two grown-up children and lives in St Albans.

The Chartered Institute of Personnel and Development is the leading publisher of books and reports for personnel and training professionals, students, and all those concerned with the effective management and development of people at work. For details of all our titles, please contact the publishing department:

Tel: 020-8263 3387

Fax: 020-8263 3850

E-mail cipd@cipd.co.uk

Published by the Chartered Institute of Personnel and Development, CIPD House, Camp Road, London, SW19 4UX

Creating a Learning and Development Strategy

The HR Business Partner's Guide to Developing People

Second edition

Andrew Mayo

Chartered Institute of Personnel and Development

First edition published 1998

This edition published 2004

© Chartered Institute of Personnel and Development, 2004

Designed and typeset by Fakenham Photosetting, Fakenham, Norfolk

Printed in Great Britain by The Cromwell Press, Trowbridge, Wiltshire

British Library Cataloguing in Publication Data
A catalogue of this publication is available from the British Library

ISBN 1 84398 056 8

Chartered Institute of Personnel and Development, CIPD House,
Camp Road, London, SW19 4UX
Tel: 020 8971 9000   Fax: 020 8263 3333
Email: cipd@cipd.co.uk   Website: www.cipd.co.uk
Incorporated by Royal Charter.   Registered Charity No. 1079797
The catalogue of all CIPD titles can be viewed on the CIPD website:
www.cipd.co.uk/bookstore

■ CONTENTS

ACKNOWLEDGEMENTS

When you focus on a subject for several months in depth, you gain tremendously as you try to think things through from first principles. But you cannot do this in isolation: you test and exchange ideas, you find out what other people have said, and you need a lot of support, encouragement and tolerance. And of course, whatever you eventually conclude is the result of many years of experience and interaction at every level with many people.

In the six years since the first edition I have pursued the subject of strategy further, interacting with many students and colleagues at Middlesex University, and learnt so much more. This edition has many changes, and my thanks go first to my colleague Karen Glasse, for her detailed and perceptive research, for her helpful comments on the final draft and for her stimulating partnership in running the CIPD courses on this subject. Geoff Atkinson helped me particularly with the '8 step method', and I continue to owe a debt to the innovations and professionalism of my ex-colleagues at ICL, where I worked for nearly 20 years.

My thanks to CIPD Publishing for their continued support, and to the anonymous people who took the trouble to review the proposals for this edition and made many valuable suggestions. Finally, it is the tolerance and understanding of those who share your life that is so essential to a project such as this – and so my special thanks once again are to my wife Elisabeth.

▪ LIST OF FIGURES

■ LIST OF TABLES

■ INTRODUCTION

Professional HR people refer to themselves today as 'business partners', and are concerned to both be 'strategic' themselves and to be involved in strategic activities. They, along with other support functions such as IT, want to feel they have a part in *shaping* the business rather than being mere supporting resources reactive to managerial demands.

In 1988 the Ashridge Management Research Group distinguished three basic models of managing HRD, with progressive levels of sophistication as follows:

■ *The fragmented approach* – an emphasis on training programmes, discrete and formalised, and unconnected particularly with business priorities.

■ *The formalised approach* – a more professional systematisation of training activitives, including pre- and post-event activities.

■ *The focused approach* – where training and development is a tool of organisational success, and activities are clearly focused towards that end.

This book is essentially about the last approach.

We now know just how important 'intangible assets' are in building value for organisations, and that pursuing value growth solely on maximising current profits is not a sustainable strategy. The major portion of the intangible asset portfolio depends on people – their capability, their knowledge and wisdom, and how they are managed and utilised. Growing intangible assets is about growing the stock of capability and knowledge in the organisation. What an exciting and critical role for Human Resources Development! And what a challenge to know just *how* such a mission can be accomplished. Nothing could be more 'strategic'.

It is six years since the first edition of this book and much has changed. The term 'e-learning' did not even appear in the index! This has emerged from its original boom to a more balanced approach, as we have learnt more about its costs and benefits. The technological hype that also drove many knowledge-management intiatives has to take second place to the reality of human behaviour, to a motivation for learning and willingness to change and adapt. Accounting scandals have, it is hoped, caused organisations to think more holistically about their future than the immediate share price. Identyifying and retaining talent has become a widespread concern. Strategy, and 'being strategic', are both over-used and misused in many contexts today, not least in the HR field. It is defined in the 1951 edition of the *Oxford Dictionary* as 'generalship, the art of war, management of an army, the art of so moving or disposing troops or ships as to impose upon the enemy the place and time and conditions for fighting preferred by oneself'. No mention of business at all here, although we can logically extrapolate the definition to that of any competitive environment. The implication is that strategy is decided by the top management, and the organisation disposes itself around its achievement. To be 'strategic', therefore, is either to be involved in the analysis and choice of options available, and/or to be *supporting* another's strategy through the use of resources. The job of Human Resource Development is to support through learning, and in so doing it needs to make its own choices of how to do that effectively.

There undoubtedly continues to be a need for a business-oriented and systematic framework to training and development. Despite the continued emphasis on the importance of learning at all levels, there are still many training and development agendas and portfolios that have far more to do with what trainers want to do than any added value to the organisation. It is very easy to convince oneself and others that a proposed activity is a *good thing* because time spent in learning of all kinds is likely to produce some benefit. Moreover, people may enjoy their experience. Professional developers by their nature tend to over-emphasise 'soft' skills development, believing perhaps that 'task' or 'technical' training will take care of itself. So we have to ask ourselves 'are we being driven seriously by identified business needs, or are we making our own interpretation of what we think the organisation needs?' This book is dedicated to help practitioners be able to answer positively to the first option of these.

The term 'HRD' will be used as an abbreviation for all activities concerned with training, learning and development. Whatever the reader's title, hopefully he or she can find a link with this generic term for the professional who is concerned with both doing the right things in training and development, and doing them in the best way. This will often be a generalist HR person whose role includes responsibility for HRD.

This second edition has been substantially rewritten, as I have learnt so much more myself through working with clients and students. It adds two new chapters – on career and continuity management and return on investment; the two appendices are also new.

Its aim is to be *useful* to practitioners at all levels. This is its only test of success: useful in making choices from options, in making decisions about what to do, and in ultimately adding value to their organisations.

1 ■ THE CONTEXT OF A PEOPLE DEVELOPMENT STRATEGY

In this chapter we place people in the overall context of organisational strategy and examine why people development is itself a vital strategic contribution. We look at the strategic process and the importance of alignment, and develop a model for preparing an HRD strategy. Finally, we think about the purposes, audiences and content of a strategy.

HUMAN CAPITAL AND ITS ROLE IN CREATING VALUE

'Human capital' is a term for people that is replacing 'human resources'. Though not a term to everybody's taste, it is one that reflects a view of people as value creating *assets* rather than primarily as costs. It is not just a new term invented by consultants or a guru – it comes from understanding how value is created in an organisation. If the HRD 'business partner' has a firm grasp of the arguments that follow, they will always have the basis of a robust discussion with the finance director.

The assets of an organisation split into two groups, the *tangible* and the *intangible*. The former are those which feature in the balance sheet, essentially financial and physical, measured according to accepted standards. The intangible are hard to measure and there are few standards for doing so. In a commercial organisation, with a value determined by a market for its shares, on average over all sectors the tangible measured part comprises only a quarter to a third of the total value. In other words, those who value shares are effectively placing much more emphasis on the intangible assets that are believed to create *sustainable* value in the future.

Intangible assets are often referred to as *intellectual capital*, and are typically broken down into three categories:

- customer or relationship capital – brands, customer relations, contracts, reputation, levels of service or provision to beneficiaries

- structural or organisational capital – know-how, patents, knowledge, systems and processes, culture

- human or competence capital – capability, experience, wisdom, and the effectiveness of leadership and teams.

Organisations of all kinds exist only to provide value for their stakeholders. For those that are commercial, the prime stakeholder group is the shareholders or owners. For nonprofit organisations it may be the beneficiaries, or governments. But there is always a network of different stakeholders, and the satisfaction of all of them is essential to meet the needs of the prime group. Figure 1.1 shows how this value is built up. It is probably not possible to assign specific monetary values to each category, which is made up of many components. But if we ask the questions:

- How is value *maintained* for stakeholders?

- How is value *grown* for stakeholders?

we can only conclude that it is people and the way they are managed that provide the driving force. Without them, value cannot be maintained or grown; intellectual capital will not grow, and the ultimate return to the prime stakeholders will neither be sustained nor enhanced.

Figure 1.1 People in the value-creating chain

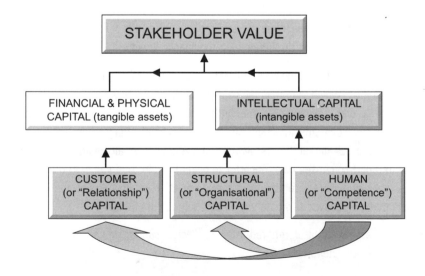

This is a dynamic scenario and people are the foundational assets in the value chain, driving through their knowledge and capability innovation in products and services, in processes and systems, and building relationships with customers. Nothing could be more strategic, therefore, than our ability to enhance and grow the competence, productivity and innovation of our human capital – or as many would prefer it, our 'people capital'.

Accountants generally force us to look at many intangible assets as costs, as they make no distinction between those that are a general expense in running the organisation, and those that are investments in the future. When we think about people development, this is an important distinction to make.

Figure 1.1 also shows we cannot look at people development in isolation from what is happening in the organisation overall. It leads to the two fundamental issues of 'alignment' of any people-development strategy with other strategies, and the importance of integration between individual and *organisational* development.

APPLICATION

What is the ratio (if available) in your organisation between the market value and the net book value on the balance sheet? Identify the main components of intellectual capital in your organisation, especially the human assets.

STRATEGIC ALIGNMENT

The great enemy of organisations, especially those that are diverse and complex, is the lack of alignment and 'connectivity' – not being 'joined-up'. From HRD's perspective, there are two challenges:

- To what extent is HRD aligned *vertically*? What does it mean to be a business partner, working with and supporting the business strategy and the managers seeking to implement it?

- To what extent is HRD aligned *horizontally*? How consistent are HRD policies and initiatives with other organisational and HR programmes?

Vertical alignment

Most HR and HRD strategies will state their desire to be 'business linked', and most professionals will describe their roles today as those of 'business partnership'. There is a great danger of lip service here, making tenuous links between what we really would like to do and suitable supporting phrases in the business plans. Because professionals in this function tend to read and network more than most, they are very conscious of the latest ideas and so-called 'best practices'. They may well believe strongly that their HR and HRD strategy is designed to benefit the organisation, but if it has been prepared in isolation by the function itself it runs the risks of nonalignment and inappropriate priorities. We can do a lot of 'things that are right', but the question is whether we are doing the 'right things'. Trainers are particularly susceptible to the trap of 'I have a great idea for the organisation' (other support functions such as IT can be as bad), and they often suffer from a lack of business knowledge and orientation as well. They have their own interests and values, and even when making an effort to seek out the needs of individuals and teams they may translate them into their preferred comfort zone of solutions. It is easy to be seduced by positive feedback from events, and in the absence of a true evaluation culture be quite unconscious of whether any real benefit is being experienced by the organisation.

Benchmarking and learning from others are valuable activities. The task of a support function, however (and we should never lose sight of the reality of this as HR's role), is to harness all the professional knowledge available to help people and people management be more effective in achieving what the organisation wants to achieve.

Different levels of alignment can be plotted along two dimensions, as in Figure 1.2. One dimension is about being *reactive* or *proactive*. Do we react to requests from managers for help, or are we regularly working with them to stimulate and suggest ideas, work out solutions together, and jointly monitor initiatives? The second dimension is whether we do this at an *operational* level or a *strategic* level? The distinction is between the

Figure 1.2 Business linkages

	Reactive	Proactive
Strategic	STRATEGIC SUPPORTER *Supporting business goals through professional HR and HRD solutions*	STRATEGIC PARTNER *Dynamic and continuous integration between HR/HRD and business goals*
Operational	OPERATIONAL SUPPORTER *Providing administrative support for management decisions*	OPERATIONAL PARTNER *Working with management to support day-to-day needs*

current day-to-day business and that which is more forward looking, and involves change from what we do today.

The characteristics of the four quadrants are as follows:

- *Reactive, operational*. This is about responding to managers' requests for training of various kinds, both for their departments and as a result of appraisals for individuals. HRD sources solutions and suppliers and meets the requests.

- *Reactive, strategic*. In this mode, HRD helps managers with their longer-term needs, responds to their business plans with appropriate supporting programmes, and develops customised learning solutions for them.

- *Proactive, operational*. The difference here is that regular meetings occur with management, keeping in touch with progress on their business goals, suggesting ideas, challenging practices and working jointly on people-capability issues.

- *Proactive, strategic*. The level of involvement is broader and longer term here. It includes contributing to and challenging business strategies, working together with the management team on organisation development initiatives, and building long-term capabilities.

It is very unlikely that any given HRD function will be operating solely in one quadrant. The question to be asked is about the balance of effort between them, and how to manage client expectations. A comprehensive people-development strategy will embrace the whole range.

Horizontal alignment

What is important here is that chosen HRD strategies and initiatives do not conflict with other initiatives, whether from HR or elsewhere.

A classic example is the use of reward systems to support (or otherwise) desired business strategies. Sales bonus plans (for example) may be constructed in such a way as to constrain desired development activities, by not providing any incentive to spend time on them. Another example is where the design of HR information systems is based on the premiss that all learning is training, and features fields to do with off-the-job training and nothing else.

In the perfect world, all organisational strategies and plans are shared between units and functions and checked for consistency. Unfortunately, few organisations meet this aspiration, and the responsible HRD director will take the initiative to ensure that the HRD strategy is aligned where needed.

▶ Table 1.1 A checklist for alignment

Role	Activities	✓?
Operational supporter	■ evaluates optimal solutions and providers for a stated need ■ prioritises within a set budget	
Operational partner	■ works with managers to analyse learning needs ■ suggests appropriate learning modes and solutions ■ receives business reports and attends business meetings ■ prepares customised solutions for identified needs ■ identifies where operational problems can be helped by learning ■ learning budget integrated with business budget	
Strategic supporter	■ evaluating specific current business goals and strategies for the capability levels needed for success ■ providing processes and programmes that will support those strategies prioritising resources based on strategic impact	
Strategic partner	■ be a member of the strategic analysis group ■ be part of the team that sets the goals and strategies ■ monitoring the value and growth of human assets in the organisation ■ working with the senior team to define values and policies in people development ■ working with the senior team to define the people and organisation development strategy ■ proposing initiatives which will lead to greater long-term effectiveness ■ justifying initiatives using ROI analysis, and preparing a strategic development budget ■ ensures initiatives are not in conflict with others	

Table 1.1 is a checklist for the involvement of the HRD function in the different roles. Since most HRD departments report into a broader HR function, it may be the higher-level HR director who is involved more in the strategic partnership arena. Frequently, he or she is excluded from any input into the substance of the business strategies themselves, and is expected to be involved only in implementation. This depends on many factors – cultural, historical, structural – but more than anything else on the calibre and business credibility of the individuals concerned. We discuss in Chapter 8 how credibility and influence can be increased.

APPLICATION

How does the checklist work for you? How many can be ticked in the right-hand column? Are there any areas you would like to address?

Rather than compete for senior management time with our own agendas, it is better to see how we can deploy our knowledge, skills and experience in people development to help achieve *their* goals.

STRATEGY AND PHILOSOPHY – THE STRATEGIC PARTNERSHIP ROLE

Millions of words have been written about strategy, and millions of hours spent studying it by executives and MBA students. For our purpose it is helpful to make a distinction between three different components.

- The 'organisational strategy' – these are the answers to the 'umbrella' questions such as:

  - 'what are we in business for'? (our mission)

  - 'what is our vision of what we want to achieve?' (our vision)

  - 'what will govern our behaviour and priorities?'(our values)

  - 'what principles will govern the way we do business?' (our business philosophy).

  One of HR's strategic partnership roles may be in the definition of these, perhaps initiating but definitely participating in the decision process and – as we shall see in Chapter 2 – HRD has a major responsibility for making them a reality.

  Once decided, these will provide a semi-permanent 'umbrella' and be changed only when the management team feels they are out of date – it may happen, for example, due to mergers and restructuring.

- The 'business strategy' – where are we trying to get to and how in the coming period (typically three to five years)? Circumstances may force rapid re-evaluation of existing strategies – such as happened to the airline industry after 11 September 2001. But generally they provide direction and guidance for the more current business *plans* and the consequent resourcing needs. Organisations vary in the complexity of their strategic planning departments and processes – some sectors

Figure 1.3 Steps in the strategic process

```
┌─────────────────────┐        ┌─────────────────────┐
│     Strategic       │        │     Strategic       │
│     Analysis        │   ⟹    │    Goal Setting     │
│                     │        │                     │
│       SWOT          │        │      Growth         │
│  Core competences   │        │ Customer satisfaction│
│ Environmental studies│       │    Profitability    │
│  Market projections │        │    Market share     │
└─────────────────────┘        └─────────────────────┘

┌─────────────────────┐        ┌─────────────────────┐
│   Implementation    │        │   Chosen Routes     │
│                     │        │    to the Goals     │
│ Leveraging resources│   ⟸    │                     │
│ Progress measurement│        │     Resources       │
│  Conflict resolution│        │ Systems & processes │
│ Change management   │        │    Capability       │
│                     │        │    Partnership      │
└─────────────────────┘        └─────────────────────┘
```

find it difficult to plan beyond the next major project or for more than a few months ahead. HRD contributes in many ways to this with programmes linked to specific objectives.

■ The 'functional strategy' – the detailed plans for a supporting function – such as HRD – on how they are going to contribute to the achievement of both the above.

Figure 1.3 shows a fairly typical set of steps in the strategic process. Although this depicts a commercial and competitive environment, the same basic steps would apply for the public or voluntary sectors.

The first step is the analysis of an organisation's position in its world. Analytical techniques abound, and are continually being invented. Perhaps most tried and trusted of all is the 'SWOT' approach – 'strengths, weaknesses, opportunities and threats'.

Then, based on whatever studies are done, goals are set for achievement. These will typically be about financial factors and market positioning, although 'softer' goals may be set relating to customers and employees. (It would not be unknown for these goals to be inconsistent with the analysis, and be fixed for political or 'macho' purposes. 'Aggressive' targets may be more acceptable than realistic ones. For example, in the 1990s the naked pursuit of 'double digit growth' – that could often not be supported by the market conditions – led to many inappropriate acquisitions that lost shareholder value for companies). The most difficult and important decision in strategy creation is to decide what *not* to do, rather than what to go for.

The next step is to choose routes to the goals. These are the *strategies* – although the word is often used to embrace the goals too. Each requires resources, processes and human capability to make them happen. The reverse arrow in Figure 1.3 represents a *reality check* – is it going to be feasible to achieve what we want with the resources and timescales available?

Lastly, all the paper and plans are useless without sound implementation. It is often said that 'Strategy is 10 per cent analysis and 90 per cent implementation'. The 's' word slips off the tongue so readily today that one hears people talk about 'implementation strategies' – meaning ways of making the real strategy actually happen! This final planning of what will be done may also necessitate a revisit of the goals.

This is a nice theoretical model. In practice, strategy is an ongoing emergent understanding of what is happening around us and adapting accordingly. So, whereas the planned directions are helpful guides, they cease to be so if not reviewed constantly in the light of the lessons being learnt daily from experience.

The role of HR and HRD in contributing to business strategy

Table 1.1 suggests that two roles could be:

- being part of the strategy *analysis* team
- being part of the strategy *decision* team.

The advantages of this are clear – first, the intimate involvement with the factors affecting the business and second, the opportunity to introduce people-related factors that may otherwise be neglected.

Whether they have this involvement or not, there is a clear role in evaluating the strategies for realism in areas (such as the law) that may have been overlooked, and also to highlight the implications for resourcing and capability. The greatest source of failure of strategy implementation is the mismatch between the desired goals and the *resources* assigned to achieve them.

When it comes to implementation, there is a major role to play in communicating and in creating understanding. In most organisations strategies are generated and decided on by top management, and may be unknown by or have little meaning for the average employee. Hay and Williamson (1997) defined a good strategy as seen from *below* as:

- providing inspiration
- helping people see the linkage between what they are doing and the rest of the company
- offering guidance on trade-offs

- giving people discretion to generate options and act

- helping communication through a common language.

The strategies of support functions should be derived from the organisation's overall strategy. They should not be prepared in parallel, except at the highest level, since they need to follow from and support the eventual business plans.

Before we go further, we cannot ignore the fact that it may be difficult to actually *find* any strategies for HR/HRD to link into. Some organisations are so short term (and consistently routine) in their business cycles that life is very 'here and now'. In this type of environment, just articulating the strategy as being 'responsive and market driven' can often help managers and employees to operate successfully. Others struggle for a long time to find the strategy to choose. If this is the case, it does not mean we cannot have an HRD strategy, since we still have people and have to decide what to do about their development. But we shall need more judgement and intuition in setting priorities than if we can link clearly to business direction.

BUSINESS STRATEGY, ORGANISATION DEVELOPMENT STRATEGIES AND HRD STRATEGY

All business strategies require an organisation strategy, to create the kind of organisation that will be most effective in delivering them. By this we mean:

- What *structure* will be most effective? Where do we want to have business units and profit (or financial) accountability? How centralised do we want support functions to be? What is the ideal number of management layers? What balance do we want between process-based teams and traditional hierarchy?

- What *systems and processes* will bind the organisation together? What will be the balance between 'global' and 'local' processes? How will knowledge be managed across the organisation?

- To what extent will we be a *learning* organisation, and what will this mean in practice?

- What *behaviours and attitudes* will characterise people in the organisation?

One of the best ways to determine the answers to these questions is to look at the organisation from a future stakeholder perspective. The question to ask is:

" Imagine our business strategies have been achieved in 20xx as planned, as each of our stakeholders looks at our organisation, what are they seeing in terms of the four questions above? 🔳🔳

This gives us an *organisational vision*, against which we can compare where we are today and build an organisation development strategy.

APPLICATION

Does your organisation have such a vision? If not, how would you go about preparing one? Do you think your answers to the questions and those of senior management would line up? Where might they be different?

Figure 1.4 indicates the connections between the various strategies. This model applies to any support function, not just HRD. It looks at three components of strategy, namely:

- where we want to be in the medium to long term

- what we are currently trying to achieve

- issues and problems that need resolution.

Figure 1.4 Linking support functions with business strategies

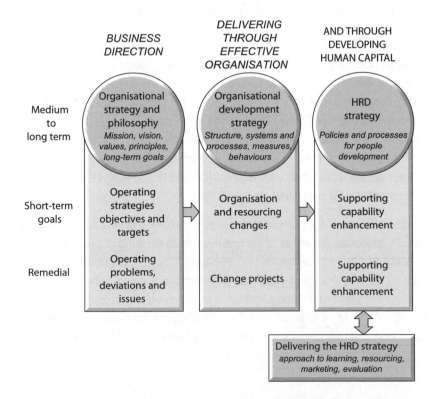

Each of these plays into organisation development and human capital development, or HRD.

The key components of an HRD strategy

The HRD strategy is composed of three parts:

1 an 'umbrella strategy', which includes approaches and policies that support the 'organisational strategy', and are semi-permanent

2 'specific strategies', which relate to the current organisational goals and issues. These fall into two categories – those that are *proactive* in terms of supporting the objectives of management, and those that are *remedial* – ie which help solve performance issues at any level.

3 a *functional* strategy for the HRD department, which represents the choices it makes in terms of its own approach to learning, to resourcing, funding, marketing, evaluation and so on. This will include both its internal choices and how it will deal with the external world of government, the community, customers and so on.

The vital links between HRD and organisation development

A large government agency spent £750,000 on an intensive executive development programme for its top 100 leaders. This generated a lot of debate and analysis of where the agency was at the time and where it should aim for. The purpose of the programme was to 'prepare the leadership for change'. After the programme was completed, the leaders returned to their jobs, in an unchanged organisation. Although there were many initiatives afoot aimed at developing a more effective organisation, nothing could be particularly related to the programme. This not untypical event raises the question of synergy between organisational development (OD) and HRD, and how HRD programmes cannot stand alone if any lasting result is sought.

Providing new knowledge, skills and behaviours will not lead to effective learning if the structure, processes and values of the organisation do not support their application in the workplace. It is a challenge for HRD managers to beware of providing events that focus on learning from best practice from other organisations when their own is incapable of embracing and applying them. It is all very well to learn about SouthWest Airlines as a model of empowerment, fun and efficiency, for example, but how many people work in an organisation where their way of working would be acceptable?

DEVELOPING HUMAN CAPITAL

The mission of HRD is to develop the human capital of the organisation, and we have seen how fundamentally strategic it is to do this. Some greater analysis of what we mean by human capital will be appropriate at this point.

The core of human capital is the individual and collective capability available to an organisation. Figure 1.5 shows the components of capability, and it is these components that HRD seeks to enhance through learning (they are expanded in Chapter 4).

■ *Values and attitudes* surround all our other capabilities and drive many of our behaviours. They are not easily changed, although some initiatives are targeted at them – eg in workplace behaviour or attitudes to customers.

■ *Qualifications* are indicators of depth of knowledge in specific areas.

■ *Experience* is about the diversity of contexts that have been experienced, the depth and variety of challenges, and particular situations.

■ *Personal skills* is the core of most 'competency frameworks' and includes a mix of behaviours derived from personality, experience and training.

■ *Know-how* covers business, technical and professional knowledge and skills.

■ *'Know-who'* is often neglected, but critical for success – the range of contacts, internal and external, that can provide information, expertise and support.

Modes of learning

People develop through:

education

Figure 1.5 A Model of Capability

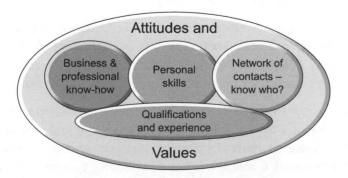

training

learning from others

experiences.

A complete learning programme, that conscientiously takes learners around the 'learning cycle', may use several or all of these modes.

Education is to do with reframing, refining, or developing the mind, and so also can affect people's attitudes and values. Under this category we would place:

- *Many general management development programmes.* Whether for individuals or for groups, the learning goals are often primarily educational – based on our definition. Other benefits are clearly present. Respondents to evaluation questionnaires find the experience very valuable for three reasons: first, the network of people with whom they have shared time; second, the time to reflect on their job; and third, the broadening of their minds giving a sounder basis for future decisions. Organisations use these to create a familiarity with common models and thinking frameworks, personal insights, to provide dialogue with senior management or to accelerate change.

- *Attitudinal change initiatives.* These would include, for example, customer orientation, total quality, multicultural awareness, managing diversity, workplace behaviour – these are primarily educational, but also designed to change behaviour within the organisation.

- *Achieving professional qualifications.* There are several pressures encouraging this. Customers may specify that they deal only with qualified personnel; governments have national targets and look for co-operation in achieving them; and employees increasingly find an appropriate qualification as a necessary entry passport. The actual benefits to the organisation are variable, and we could legitimately class much of what is done in this area of learning as part of the HR benefits strategy rather than of a training and development strategy.

Training is concerned with enhancing both know-*how* (for specialised knowledge and skills in business, technical and professional areas) and with developing personal skills. It is generally true that training needs opportunities for speedy application and consolidation in the workplace, and without this its effects are dissipated.

Learning from others is a powerful learning mode and includes coaching and mentoring. The former is built around a specific learning need; the latter is used more for broader, longer-term development. Much of what is currently termed 'coaching,' especially using external professionals, is more akin to mentoring. Coaching does not have to be seen only as manager–employee help; a person can receive coaching from anyone around them, even a subordinate.

Learning from experiences is the most potent learning of all, as research has clearly shown. This includes not only job rotation and career progression, but the use of secondments, projects, task force membership, delegation, broadening of responsibilities, and so on. 'Action learning' is a broad term embracing these, and also the sharing of experiences with others. Learning 'assignments' are usefully designed and used to apply specifically what has been learnt from the other modes. One does not come back from a leadership course and say ' I am now a leader'. What such a course does is to provide a framework for understanding what leadership is about and within which to experiment and act. This requires live real-time opportunity for the learning to take place.

This book is entitled *Creating a Learning and Development Strategy*. The distinction here is not precise, as 'development' may deploy all the modes of learning. Generally it refers to the longer-term investment in people. Development takes time. The essence of managing people *development* (whether managed by individuals themselves or with the help of others) is to provide and benefit from opportunities, and most of these will be new experiences.

APPLICATION

If you look at the learning programmes operating in your organisation today, how would you classify them in relation to the four ways of developing capability? How do your present activities split between them? Does the balance feel right?

A MODEL FOR CREATING AN HRD STRATEGY

Before we introduce the basic model framework used in this book, we need to look at the distinction between 'strategy' and 'plans', as this often causes confusion. We discussed earlier different business linkages using the terms 'strategic' and 'operational'. It could be argued that an HRD strategy is concerned only with the bigger, long-term picture. However, this would have limited use for the practitioner who is engaged in all the linkages. We are therefore going to combine both together under the heading of 'strategy', acknowledging that part of it will be operational and renewable as business objectives and needs change. Indeed, one of the greatest challenges for HRD is to manage the balance of delivering both the proactive and the reactive, the operational and the strategic, and to be flexible along with the plans.

Figure 1.6 Drivers of the HRD Strategy

The framework for the 'drivers' or 'contributors' to an HRD strategy is shown in Figure 1.6; this expands the general model of Figure 1.4 and the three parts referred to.

APPLICATION

Adapt the model of Figure 1.6 for your organisation using your own internal language.

The medium/long-term part of the strategy is the overall approach to people development. This is more or less permanent and provides support for the ongoing organisational strategy. The first set of five drivers comprises:

1 The *mission, vision, values and goals* of the organisation – where stated clearly and publicly. The questions for HRD are: What should we be doing to progress the organisation towards its vision? How should HRD both demonstrate the values and embed them into everyday behaviours?

2 Many corporate strategies will define the *principles and beliefs* of people management – how will HRD support these, through its policies and processes? These may or may not be explicit, but they will certainly exist, and will significantly

influence our approach to *development*, as well as certain kinds of training and education.

3 There is the need to maintain, and enhance, what the organisation is really good at doing – its *core competences* we might say. Thus, if we are in the oil exploration business we are continually going to focus on generating and sharing knowledge to do with hydrology, drilling technology and production processes, because these are fundamental to our business. In a competitive world, we may have expertise and methodologies that are closely guarded in these 'core' areas, and we probably will not want to outsource these, but develop them internally.

4 As discussed above, HRD needs to support the *OD strategy*, and the longer-term changes that this embraces.

5 The *external environment* must be taken into account. Political, economic, social, legal and technological changes may influence our approaches to people development, particularly if we work in a public sector enterprise.

These drivers lead us to *policies, processes and programmes*, which we shall keep under review but which otherwise will apply beyond the current year. (They are discussed further in Chapter 2, and provide the basic strategic framework for HRD.) There is, of course, nothing in organisations today that can be described as 'permanent'; they need to be continually learning and adaptable to change. However, constant changes in direction and approach cause confusion and make it difficult to achieve the benefits that come from many longer-term development programmes. As illustrated clearly in the book *Built to Last* by American researchers Porras and Collins (1994), long-term success is directly related to consistency of vision, beliefs and cultural approaches.

Current business strategies and operations provide us with the second and third sets of drivers. The first set is about being *proactive* in terms of supporting the objectives of management in achieving their current goals. Being proactive implies discussions with each operating unit within the cope of the HRD director, to see how learning initiatives will support them. The goals and strategies in the current plan all have implications for the capability of divisions, teams and the people in them. Let's say we have a goal to double our sales turnover. How is this going to be achieved?; by new products?; or new geographies?; by salespeople?; by acquisition?; or by new distribution channels? Whatever the strategy is, people are involved, and success or failure depends on their ability to deliver. In addition to overt business goals, specific units may be planning changes in the way they do things – cultural, structural or in systems and processes. These will certainly require support from HRD.

Current *organisational and human resource plans* also require proactive action. Many reorganisations are put together with little thought for the capability needed to make them work – until afterwards. Many a workshop on 'matrix management' for example is *remedial*. The main goal seems to be to create some semblance of rationality on paper, slotting people into the positions created. The HRD director should ideally be involved in all reorganisations to be able to advise on the capability issues that will need to be addressed. Human resource plans are also critical – beyond headcount figures from the business plans, and focused on flows into, out of and within the organisation. Plans should also define *quantities* of skills, in the requirements for different skill levels.

Every organisation has problems, and most problems when analysed find their causes in either systems and processes or in the capability of people, teams and individuals. We may have problems with safety, with customer service, with productivity, or a host of other shortfalls. Appraisal discussions lead to learning needs for individuals. This set of drivers we can call *remedial* – ie helping to solve performance issues at any level. *External changes* also arise, demanding a speedy response – changes in regulations, in the law, or other factors in the environment in which the organisation operates.

These two categories lead to a host of demands that have to be prioritised. HRD has a ready tendency to be reactive, especially when its help is actively sought. It is often so tied up in maintaining its 'umbrella framework' and in reacting to demands that the second category of proactive support takes last priority. This is a common failing of many strategies and plans, often attributable to discomfort and unfamiliarity with the hard facts of daily business life.

All the above is about *what* HRD should do. A systematic analysis of all the drivers will give HRD a proper balance of *top-down* needs and *bottom-up* needs, that a traditional 'training needs analysis' may not do. In addition to the ongoing policies, processes and programmes, the second and third categories will give us a specific set of learning initiatives. These are expanded on in Chapter 3.

Finally, HRD has to make its own choices as to *how* it will deliver the needed learning – its own 'functional strategy'. It needs to have its set of beliefs about how people learn, and how it will design learning programmes. It will need to divide the organisation into *populations* who share common processes and have similar types of learning needs – such as senior management or the technical support people. It will need to decide on the *methodologies* it will use, such as e-learning and evaluation; and its *resources, roles* and *funding*. There is always politics in organisations, and it will need strategies for *involvement* of others, *marketing* and *communication*. Reaching out to all levels and all units, HRD is inevitably pulled in different directions. How does it choose who and where it needs to influence in the organisation? How does it position and market its services? And lastly, HRD must determine how it will *measure* and*monitor* its own effectiveness.

All these decisions and choices will affect the function's ability to deliver its own mission of supporting the organisation through developing human capital. They will take account of good professional practices learnt from others, but be applied with care. Chapters 4–8 discuss these issues.

STRATEGY DOCUMENTATION

At the end of this section, we outline some actual organisational strategy documents, and they are very diverse. There is no universal answer, and many practitioners will already have a corporate format to adhere to. However, it helps to be clear about:

- *the purpose* – why are we doing it and what will it be used for?
- *the audience* – who will see it and what message do we want to convey?
- *the format* – what will be included?
- *the process of creation* – how we shall put it together.

The purpose

Many HRD functions could not provide one document detailing strategies and plans coherently, but nevertheless could give various documents that describe different things that they do, and the part that managers or employees should play in development. Why would one take the trouble to produce a comprehensively documented strategy? There are a number of possible reasons:

- as part of an organisational strategic planning process that requires a set of coherent integrated strategies from all activities – including HR/HRD
- as a vehicle for consultation/discussion with line management about training and development issues
- as a means of communicating to staff beliefs, policies and plans
- for managing expectations in people development
- as a means of linking HRD activities systematically with business needs
- for establishing priorities and plans for HRD activities and resources
- for achieving an approved and authoritative framework for HRD policies and activities
- as a means of 'zero-basing' current activity and recalibrating what we are doing in HRD, and how

- for securing budgets and resources

- for demonstration to external bodies that required standards are being met

- for influencing change

- for internal visibility and credibility

- for providing integration across disparate units

- for external publicity.

It is highly likely that one or more of these reasons exist, and that disciplined systematic thinking and presentation will achieve the particular goal that is sought. We need to establish clearly why the strategy is being created, or reviewed, and what we should like to achieve with it.

▷ Table 1.2 Audiences for a strategy document

Type of audience	Goals of communication	Content emphasis
Chief executives	Commitment, involvement	Executive summary, business links, personal commitments needed
HR directors	Approval, resources	Business links, professional methodology, resources, costs
Strategic planners	Process completion	Meeting requirements, links to business and other strategies
Line managers	Involvement, partnership	Processes, roles, involvement
HRD staff	Commitment, participation	Priorities, skills, plans
All employees	Information, participation	Policies, directions, plans
HR business partners	Support, co-operation	Processes, roles, involvement
Trade union/staff reps	Support, co-operation	Concern for people
External assessors	Approval	Meeting standards required
External committees	Approval	Meeting external interest
Fund providers	Approval, resources	Meeting funds criteria
Other organisations	Publicity, image, reputation	Professionalism, leading-edge practices
Potential recruits	Employee image, desirability	Beliefs, policies, relevant programmes

The audience

All communications should be tailored for their audience, and this will depend on their purpose. An HRD strategy may have several different audiences. Table 1.2 shows some of them, with possible goals of communication, and the consequent emphasis on content.

Thus there is a great diversity of requirement. Not all potential audiences will need every part of the strategy and plans, and some will need parts of it especially tailored to their needs. The strategy will be constructed in modules reflecting these needs, and parts can be drawn from it as appropriate. Each audience will have its own *summary* at the front, which should address any concerns they are likely to have, focus on their interests and how they will be provided for, and also the key messages or commitments that HRD wants from them.

APPLICATION

Which audiences exist in your organisation for an HRD strategy? List them in approximate order of priority. What would you like your strategy to achieve with each of them?

The format

Table 1.3 suggests the kind of headings that would support our model. Each organisation will need to devise its own format, but this may prove a helpful checklist. These headings may not necessarily all be in one document or in the order suggested in the table. Arguably, however, they should be found *somewhere* – that is, HRD has thought through all these issues and worked out where they should be.

The process of creation

Few practitioners will start from scratch. They will inherit existing policies, processes, traditions and requirements. Many of these will continue to be valid. However, the process of taking the model of Figure 1.6 and going systematically through the various components is always valuable – asking these questions about everything that is done currently:

- Is this meeting the organisation's needs successfully?
- Does it fit comfortably within the priorities of today's strategies?
- Should it be eliminated, replaced or re-engineered?

▷ Table 1.3 Possible constituents of an HRD strategy

Introduction

1   Executive summary

2   Statement of purpose and the audience(s) for the strategy

Part One

3   Statement of organisational beliefs concerning people development and learning

4   External factors influencing approaches to people development

5   Mission of HRD; its own strategic goals

6   HRD policy framework

7   Organisational mission, vision, goals and core competences – how HRD will support them

8   Aspects of OD strategy needing HRD support and how this will be carried out

9   Ongoing processes and programmes that will provide the main learning and development infrastructure; their objectives

Part Two

10   Specific initiatives supporting unit business goals and strategies, organisational and change plans

11   Specific initiatives aimed at resolving operational problems

12   Specific external issues requiring a response

Part Three

13   Principles governing the HRD department; own mission statement if desired

14   HRD organisation; resources and budget needed

15   Role, responsibilities and skills for HRD and others

16   Communication and marketing plans

17   Activity and schedule plans

18   Standards of performance; measuring and monitoring effectiveness

At least annually, or when new operational business plans are instigated, Part Two of Table 1.3 needs re-evaluating. (A methodology for taking business goals and evaluating the associated learning goals is described on pages 67–68, and this needs considerable consultancy skills).

The process of building up the strategy may be used as a powerful intervention in the organisation's thinking about people development. Most managers do not give a lot of daily thought to this area of organisational life. So for the HRD director or his/her delegate to hide away in a corner and produce a magnificent document may be satisfying, but be both a missed opportunity and dangerous. The danger lies in the natural idealism of people developers, and the fact that they may miss some critical requirements for the organisation. Here are some mechanisms for involving others:

- asking top management teams to articulate their beliefs about people development (see the instrument in Figure 2.2)

- discussion and involvement with corporate strategic planning departments

- discussions with individual line management or line management teams about business priorities and performance issues

- focus groups with cross-sections of staff

- meetings with HR business partners

- 'If you were HRD manager, what would be your priorities' – interviews, discussion or questionnaires with different groups.

Such dialogues should always start with a 'bridge' to what is important for the individual or group concerned.

APPLICATION

Think of some areas (or people) that seem to have less interest in the role and activities of HRD than others. What is particularly important to them, and therefore what methods could you use to get them more involved?

Appendix A provides a 'template' for creating a strategy document.

Example strategy documents

Some research was carried out to see what a cross-section of organisations actually had by way of documentation. A number that were contacted said, with some embarrassment, that they did not have one, or were 'working on it'. However, some examples were impressive.

W F Electrical

This company has documentation as part of its HR strategy, and it begins with a comprehensive SWOT analysis. This leads to several strategic 'themes', each of which is developed into 'enablers' and 'desired results'. Each of these is expanded into objectives, actions proposed, and measures of success. The themes include sales capability, management capability and performance management.

Skanska

This is a global construction company based from Sweden with some 76,000 employees. The HR and HRD strategy for the UK Division covers the following headings:

- key business issues, followed by the HR and learning implications for each
- the actions to be taken in respect of the implications
- the resources and support needed
- project/programme plans and dates
- who is responsible
- relevant comments
- how it will be evaluated.

Large retail bank

This starts with an Introduction that restates the company's "People Strategy Objectives" for three years ahead. The next chapter is entitled "Goals and Objectives", with one over-riding goal as 'Investment in learning for all our people and our business to enable them to grow and prosper together'. Nine objectives follow, a mixture of longer-term cultural goals and specific programmes to be delivered. This is followed by a third section, which lists nine priorities. This is then backed up by a detailed implementation plan, and finally a list of roles and responsibilities.

Oxfam

This charity's learning and development strategy has 15 pages and starts with the context of the organisational strategy and its implications for learning. It summarises the desired culture and core competencies, and defines the key roles of learning and development. It goes on to summarise key principles in people development, as follows:

- Oxfam requires learning and development to be relevant to its emerging needs and strategic plans and to be consistent with its desired organisational culture.

- All learning and development interventions are opportunities to promote Oxfam's desired organisational culture. The design of learning opportunities, the behavioural models used, and the people involved in learning delivery need to be Oxfam based and must reflect the desired and emerging organisational culture.

- Line managers have primary responsibility for promoting and supporting learning and development. This is part of their day-to-day management of performance.

- Oxfam's approach to learning and development will be based upon the principles of adult learning and self-directed/self-managed learning. Learning needs and development needs will be identified with and through line managers.

- Oxfam recognises the importance of integrating a learning and development cycle into its organisational cycle.

■ Learning and development, although customised to the individual, must be managed within a systematic, organisation-wide strategy.

The document then lists three-year objectives, followed by detailed deliverables on each. Appendices comprehensively summarise the roles of key players in HRD, including managers, and list 'adult learning principles'.

Hertfordshire County Council

This council had in 1997 (now superceded by a wider "people strategy") 'Corporate Training and Development Strategy in the form of a four-page handout, clearly and professionally printed. Its overall strategy is defined under three 'beliefs':

■ The development of all our staff is central to the achievement of the Council's strategic intent.

■ We will support people so that they welcome and can cope with the changes which we need to make. This will underpin all our development activities.

■ Success will only be achieved by releasing and realising the potential of the people we employ.

The context of change is described, and a number of specific ones enumerated. This then leads to five key issues that form the basis of the strategy:

■ how to create a development and learning culture within the council

■ how to develop managers for the future

■ how to respond to the County Agenda (ie the County's overall strategy)

■ how to develop staff to meet the demands of competition

■ how to respond to the national targets for education and training and to NVQs.

Finally, actions – and in some cases policies – are enumerated on each of these five issues.

The accompanying communication and 'development charter' for employees is reproduced in Figure 8.1.

BT

The well-known telecommunications company summarises its strategy broadly as:

"Critical to the future success of the company is our ability to view our people at the forefront of change and to invest in our people – the company's 'heart' through:

■ developing new wave skills and capabilities

- providing innovative and flexible employment solutions

- encouraging and helping our people to acquire the knowledge they need to succeed in the 'new world'

- creating Internet thinking and applications at the centre of everything we do."

Leading financial services company

This company has an overall development strategy based on the learning organisation model described by Mayo and Lank in *The Power of Learning* (1994).

A team of senior executives identified six key business processes used as drivers for the major strands of HRD strategy. These strands are explained on a 'two by two' diagram, with one axis being 'Organisation/Individual' and the other 'Today/Tomorrow'; within each quadrant are key HRD activities. Thus the quadrant 'Tomorrow/Individual' includes career management and succession planning. The quadrants are built around a central core, which includes values, behaviours and performance management.

Johnson & Johnson

In the 1990s, this health care company has a document entitled 'Training and Development Strategy', with some interesting features. It began with 'Benefits of an employee training strategy', which had eight bullet points. There followed a 'Mission' and a 'Policy statement':

   ❝ The company will ensure that each employee is trained to carry out the tasks required of them. Further, the company will encourage each employee to develop his/her skills consistent with the needs of customer-driven continuous improvement and their own individual needs and aspirations. ❞

There followed a 'Summary of the relationship between business strategy and employee training strategy', a summary of the links and drivers, and then 'Seven steps of the employee training strategy'. These were in fact steps in systematic training management. 'Roles in training' came next, followed by 'Eight objectives of the training and development strategy'.

AstraZeneca

The company has a business-owned people strategy, which is being implemented over three years. It focuses on organisational behaviours, leadership development, talent management, optimising performance and professional capabilities.

The business drivers are described as:

- 'build the talent base'
- 'become an employer of choice'
- 'become one of the world's great companies'.

The global learning and development strategy was developed by the Global L&D Network and confirmed by a senior line management steering process. Its key strands are:

- *Leadership.* Drive the development of the AstraZeneca leadership capabilities at all levels of the organisation to create a unifying culture.

- *Development of a learning culture.* Promote the development of culture where every individual lives the AZ values and openly supports their colleagues learning, both from successes and mistakes.

- *Promoting self-awareness.* Promote a strong self-development and self-awareness approach, resulting in clarity of learning so that individuals optimise their full potential and leadership abilities.

- *Action learning.* Promote a team-oriented innovative environment where we use enquiry and reflection to help each other solve business problems.

- *High performance.* Provide exceptional tools and training solutions to drive a high-performance culture both globally and locally.

- *Measures.* Provide measures to ensure T&D supports business performance.

APPLICATION

What form of documentation would meet the needs of your organisation and be consistent with its culture? Draw up a specification for the headings you would use in the documents you choose.

IN BRIEF

- Organisations exist to provide and build value for their stakeholders. It is people and their capability that is the foundation stone of the value chain, through the growth of intangible assets. Nothing could be more strategic than maximising the capability of people – our 'human capital'.

- Any functional strategy must be *aligned* – synergistic with the organisation's strategies and with other functional strategies. Alignment can be strategic and operational, reactive and proactive.

■ An organisation has three levels of strategy – its 'organisational strategy' – what it is and what it wants to achieve; its 'business strategy' – what it is currently aiming for; and 'functional strategies' – supporting operational plans to help the business strategy happen.

■ The core model for an HRD strategy is in three parts – an 'umbrella' of policies and core programmes that support the organisational strategy; a series of initiatives that support the business goals; and HRD's own functional strategy.

■ HRD is about developing human capital through growing capability. Capability has several components, and can be grown by education, training, learning from others and learning from experiences.

■ What would a strategy look like? This depends on the purpose(s) and audience(s). We may have several components or versions, consistent with one another, but designed to communicate the right messages to their recipients.

REFERENCES AND FURTHER READING

BOXALL P. and PURCELL J. (2003) Strategy and Human Resource Management. Palgrave MacMillan.

CASNER-LOTTO J. (1988) Successful Training Strategies: Twenty-six innovative corporate models. San Francisco, Jossey Bass.

DAVENPORT T.O. (1999) Human Capital. San Francisco, Jossey Bass.

EDVINSSON L. and MALONE M.S. (1997) Intellectual Capital. London, Piatkus.

GAUCI P. (1988) Continuous Development: The way ahead. Ashridge Management Research Group.

HAY M. and WILLIAMSON P. (1997) 'Good strategy: The view from below'. Long Range Planning. Vol. 30, No. 5, December. pp651–664.

KOCH R. (2000) The Financial Times Guide to Strategy. 2nd edn. FT/Prentice Hall.

LABOVITZ G. and ROSANSKY V. (1997) The Power of Alignment. Wiley.

MABEY C. and SALAMAN G. (1996) Strategic Human Resource Management. London, Blackwell.

MAYO A.J. (2001) The Human Value of the Enterprise: Valuing people as assets. London, Nicholas Brealey.

MAYO A.J. *and* LANK E. (1994) *The Power of Learning.* London, IPD.

PORRAS J.I. *and* COLLINS J.C. (1994) *Built to Last.* New York, Harpers Press.

REAY D.G. (1994) *Planning a Training Strategy.* London, Kogan Page.

SLOMAN, M.A. (1994) *Handbook for Training Strategy.* London, Gower.

2 ■ THE GENERAL OR 'UMBRELLA' STRATEGY

This chapter concentrates on Part One of the HRD strategy, which provides the umbrella framework for deciding what our core policies, processes and programmes should be, and which is semi-permanent. We start off by considering the driving factors to be taken into account and go on to look at how principles of people development should be publicised, how we divide the organisation into populations with common learning interests, make decisions about policies, and some of the processes and tools we shall need.

THE FIVE DRIVERS OF THE GENERAL STRATEGY

In Chapter 1 we identified the following:

■ mission, vision, values and long-term goals

■ beliefs and principles of people management

■ core competences

■ the OD strategy

■ external factors and influences.

We shall now expand these and look at how HRD supports them.

MISSION, VISION, VALUES AND LONG-TERM GOALS

Once decided, these are generally semi-permanent and have some stability and continuity. They are statements of what an organisation *is* or what *it wants to be*. Many organisations go to great lengths to refine statements of one kind or another; others do nothing at all. However, if they exist and are to be taken seriously, then HRD must ask how they are going to be supported and become the desired reality.

Mission and vision statements can be both confused and confusing. At worst they can be convoluted lengthy paragraphs, or banal meaningless dreams that have little grasp on the hearts and minds of employees. A mission statement should describe *what business we are in* or *what we are*. It should not of itself include grand goals and ambitions but be clear and simple. It is sometimes referred to as a 'statement of purpose'.

Here are some examples from world-class companies:

❝ The purpose of Motorola is to honorably serve the community by producing products and services of superior quality at a fair price to our customers; to do this so as to earn an adequate profit which is required for the enterprise to grow, and by so doing provide the opportunity for our employees and shareholders to achieve their reasonable personal objectives. ❞

This example does not actually state what business Motorola is in. It is a commonly used format that tries to balance the satisfaction of key stakeholders.

Dilbert (see References and Further Reading for website) describes mission statements as: 'a long and awkward statement that demonstrates management's inability to think clearly'. Here are some simpler, punchier statements:

❝ We are in the business of preserving and improving human life. All of our actions must be measured by our success in achieving this goal ❞
(Merck)

❝ To enable people and businesses throughout the world to realise their full potential ❞
(Microsoft)

❝ To give ordinary folk the chance to buy the same things as rich people ❞
(Walmart)

Here is an example of a departmental statement that is very clear as to what its purpose is:

❝ The University Libraries are the scholarly information center for the University. In support of the University's mission of educational excellence, the Libraries collect, organize, preserve, and facilitate access to scholarly resources in all formats; support teaching, learning, and research in an intellectually open environment; and provide instruction in the use of traditional and new information resources and technologies. ❞

(Wright State University Libraries)

How does HRD support a mission statement? A clear statement will help to define the major core competencies needed to make the organisation a winner in its chosen field. For example, in the case of the university library, there are clear pointers to the needed staff capabilities.

Further direction may be given through vision statements, statements of direction, strategic intent, corporate goals/objectives and corporate strategies. These are distinguished from mission, purpose and values by being time related. At a corporate level they may be very general; as they are cascaded through business units they become more precise, and (should) impact on the work of units, teams and individuals.

A vision statement is a long-term goal. Sometimes it is described as a dream – as in the World Bank, which describes its dream as 'a world free of poverty'. The purpose of a vision is to be inspirational and, at least potentially, achievable but sufficiently stretching that it could not be reached in the short term. Hamel and Pralahad (1989) used the words 'strategic intent', which seem to convey the sense of vision well. One of the most famous of all was that of Komatsu in the 1970s, which was simply 'Kill Caterpillar!' Every employee saw this on the doormat as they entered work every day, and there was no difficulty in both remembering or embracing it. It was a part of everyday life. In contrast, others clearly have longwinded paragraphs that have been put together by committees.

The benefit of a vision is shown simply in this anecdote; if employees can see the big picture, they will do their part with an understanding of the system to which they belong.

❝ Three stone cutters were asked about their jobs.
The first said he was paid to cut stones.
The second replied that he used special techniques to shape stones in an

exceptional way, and proceeded to demonstrate his skills.
The third stone cutter just smiled and said 'I build cathedrals'. **⟩⟩**

This parody of vision statements illustrates the same point:

Evolution of a vision statement by cathedral builder

⟨⟨ We are building a great cathedral.
Our aim is to build the greatest cathedral in Christendom, to the greater glory of God.
By striving to become Europe's leading construction group we aim to build a cathedral that offers value for money as well as spiritual enhancement for worshippers, is environmentally healthy and will generate handsome returns on the investment in terms of increased attendance at services and associated increases in revenues. **⟩⟩**

Companies today are more explicit in their statements of what they want to achieve than the simplistic vision statement. Pressure on environmental policies, corporate governance and strategic goals, combined with the importance of the Internet as a communication means, has led to much more openness on the part of both public and private organisations.

Here is one vision statement:

⟨⟨ We believe in an 'all communicating' world. Voice, data, images and video are conveniently communicated anywhere and anytime in the world, increasing both quality-of-life, productivity and enabling a more resource-efficient world.
We are one of the major progressive forces, active around the globe, driving for this advanced communication to happen.
We are seen as the prime model of a networked organization with top innovators and entrepreneurs working in global teams. **⟩⟩**

(Ericsson)

Arch rivals Nokia use the term 'strategic intent', which is really more of a mission statement:

⟨⟨ Nokia takes a leading brand-recognised role in creating the Mobile Information Society by (a) combining Mobility and the Internet and (b) stimulating the creation of new services. **」」**

Retailer Kingfisher describes its vision as:

❝❝ Kingfisher's plan is to create an integrated, international dedicated home improvement business that combines international scale with local marketing and operational skills. The Group will concentrate on organic growth opportunities in Europe and Asia where it already has, or can establish, market leading positions. **」」**

Kingfisher's vision used to be 'To be Europe's leading retailer'. In order for people to identify with a vision, and find it helpful, it needs to be focused, measurable and at some point realistically achievable. Statements that refer just to being 'the best' or 'number one' or 'the leading company' in an arena need to be qualified. Leading *how* – in size, quality, service, innovation? Best in *what*? If we do not do that, we cannot have any sense of where we are in relation to the end goal and what kind of gaps we have to close to achieve it.

Dana Corporation, a US company in the motor supply industry, publishes its explicit corporate goals, with targets on financial return, innovation, culture and training, market share and value added services. For example:

❝❝ The Dana Style will be fully implemented creating an environment that encourages creativity and innovation at all levels: **」」**

- strengthened by diversity
- 2 ideas per person per month with 80 per cent implemented
- 40 hours of education per person per year."

Barclays Bank outlines its mission statement – which is more like a vision:

❝❝ We aspire to be one of the most admired financial services organisations in the world, recognised as an innovative, customer-focused company that delivers superb products and services, ensures excellent careers for our people and contributes positively to the communities in which we live and work. **」」**

It then goes on to describe its strategy, followed by 'how we'll do it' and – unusually – 'what we won't do'.

HRD supports the vision by communicating and explaining it, and by relevant staff having the expertise to achieve it. The methodology described in the next chapter ('eight steps') can be used to check on the necessary capability levels needed to make both the vision and strategic goals a reality. If the vision is to be the leading customer choice in the sector, we should identify who is involved in influencing customer choice and ensure they have the best possible expertise in this area. 'Leading' means 'top class knowledge and skills' in our people. HRD should also keep track of the progress being made towards the vision and the goals. What measures are being used to track towards it and how is the organisation doing? If progress is inadequate, HRD should find out why and see whether there are issues of capability holding the organisation back.

WHAT ABOUT ORGANISATIONAL VALUES?

In continuing to describe what kind of organisation we should like to be, we may support our mission statement with a statement of business philosophy and/or values. Values help to articulate a philosophy and standards of behaviour that should characterise the way the company and its people operate. They provide part of the 'corporate glue' and common language that binds a diverse corporation together and makes the corporate name stand for something in their own sector. Values may be encapsulated in a booklet that lays them out systematically, perhaps with a set of management principles as well, and termed 'The XXX Way'. Hewlett Packard was probably the originator of this approach, and many have followed in their footsteps. The 'Nokia Way' is described in detail on their website, incorporating their four values of continuous learning, achievement, customer satisfaction and respect for the individual.

Porras and Collins in *Built to Last* (1994) emphasise very strongly the value of a core ideology, which they define as 'core values' + 'purpose'. Core values are defined as:

> ❝ the organisation's essential and enduring tenets – a small set of guiding principles; not to be confused with specific cultural or operating practices; not to be compromised for financial gain or short term expediency. ❞

They are permanent. One of the tests to be made is whether the *written* values and the *unwritten* values of what is actually acceptable 'around here' actually match. Often this is not the case; and if the former have been articulated, it is always useful to test the latter against them from time to time.

Ricardo Semler, in his book *Maverick* (1994) – which describes how as a CEO he turned traditional management thinking on its head – asserts that organisations cannot have values, only people do. Nevertheless, the people in an organisation can work together, and act towards their customers or public, to some common standards of behaviour. Stated values, discussed, understood and adopted, can help to guide that behaviour. Again, attempts to create values often fail because there are too many to remember, they are too vague to be meaningful, or they lack reinforcement of any significant kind in the daily life of the organisation. Worst of all, top management does not take them seriously in its decisions. They become no more than a wish-list without a coherent plan to make them a living reality.

Values may be used as a yardstick for challenging individual or organisational behaviour, for clarifying expectations, for guiding decisions and resolving conflicting demands, and in establishing reputation and image. When subsidiary business units design their own set of values, they will take precedence over the corporate ones if they exist. Unless they are *additions* to the corporate set, this does create confusion and negate their original purpose.

It is always an important test of the currency and meaning of corporate values to see how many can recite them. Often they were produced in an era of enthusiasm for renewal, or by a previous management team, and they have lost their significance in current everyday life. Companies with a strong culture invest time in every new employee to help them to understand their values and ways of working.

Here are a few examples of values:

BT Group has these:

      ❝ Trustworthy: we do what we say we will
        Helpful: we work as one team
        Inspiring: we create new possibilities
        Straightforward: we make things clear
        Heart: we believe in what we do **❞**

Fortum, the finish energy company, captures its values in metaphors.

❝ We at Fortum have recognised four key values as a basis of our operations:

- excellent business performance

- creativity and innovation

- co-operative spirit

- high ethics

A Fortum employee who follows our common values acts with a *cool head, warm heart, open mind, and clean hands.* 🙿

▌ APPLICATION

Look for opportunities to test individuals at different levels on their memory of organisational mission, vision and value statements, and their ability to describe what they mean to them personally in their everyday work. Be open to the messages they may give regarding HRD's role in helping them to do so.

How would HRD support sets of values? Such statements, like the examples above, have enormous implications for the culture, processes and capabilities in an organisation. HRD should:

- seek to be a role model of putting them into practice itself; they will form a core consideration in HRD's own internal strategy

- apply the values in defining its organisational beliefs about people development and consequent policies and processes

- examine how it helps people in the organisation to be *competent* in the application of the values to their everyday work, making them a living reality.

Let us take as an example the common value of 'teamwork'. What exactly do we expect to see when teamwork is alive and well and a feature of our behavioural landscape? We should first define the behavioural characteristics of teams and individuals, and choose or devise a diagnostic instrument that can test the reality (through collecting perceptions). Gaps between reality and the ideal will help to set our learning objectives. We then apply this instrument to the HRD function itself, and create ongoing events that help others to explore the application to themselves. 'Values in Action' workshops (or similar), plus specific events related to each value, would be regular offerings, and a key part of our 'umbrella' strategy.

▌ APPLICATION

If you have a set of values explicit in your organisation, which of your programmes and events directly support one or more of them? How does HRD live the values through its own ways of operating?

BELIEFS AND PRINCIPLES OF PEOPLE MANAGEMENT

It may be that our corporate strategy has a section on people or people management. If so, it should be created by the senior management team and *not* by the HR function, as it is vital to have their ownership. Few senior teams have sat down to consider what they believe is right for their organisation, although their decisions and priorities in fact show where they stand, and employees have their own perceptions of what they think top management believes. Porras and Collins in *Built to Last* (1994), referred to earlier, found the following:

■ Long-lasting companies develop and promote insiders in preference to hiring outsiders.

■ A high profile charismatic leader is not required to create and run visionary companies.

■ Clear unequivocal cultural beliefs symbolise continued success.

Smith and Nephew, the global health care company created such a set, as given in Figure 2.1.

Figure 2.1 Smith and Nephew's "Management Principles"

SMITH AND NEPHEW: "MANAGEMENT PRINCIPLES"
Our company will succeed through its people
Our published values,

PERFORMANCE   **INNOVATION**   **TRUST**

set challenging standards for the way we manage at every level and in every part of the Smith and Nephew world

---

Management at all levels have the responsibility for defining and implementing policies, programmes and training to achieve these standards. In so doing however all managers in Smith and Nephew subscribe to a company-wide belief that our

• clearly communicated goals and performance standards
• an open constructive relationship with managers and supervisors
• the training, information and authority needed to do a good job
• fair recognition and reward based on performance
• equality of opportunity based on merit
• encouragement to learn and progress
• respect and dignity at all times
• encouragement to participate fully in the quest for continuous improvement

Group Executive Committee   July 2001

There are many examples of CEOs who have their own personal passion for learning. John Browne of BP is a tremendous champion of every kind of learning and knowledge sharing, and the *Harvard Business Review* carried a comprehensive interview with him (Prokesch and Browne 1998). John Towers, erstwhile chief executive of the Rover Group Ltd, and in 1996 Chair of the Business Council of the World Initiative on Lifelong Learning, wrote the following Foreword to a well-known book on lifelong learning (Longworth and Davies 1996):

❝ We at the Rover Group Ltd are proud to be among the world's foremost 'Learning Organisations' ... The strength of a company lies in the strengths of its people, and if people are underachieving the company is also underachieving ... we established the Rover Learning Business across all divisions, a learning company within a company increasingly in need of learning, and we invested in the empowerment of the people who work for us. I am glad to say that this strategy has worked like a dream. People at Rover are infinitely more fulfilled, more mature, more committed and more prepared to take responsibility than they were five years ago. ❞

Despite the demise of the company in the harsh world of car manufacture, there was still truth in his words.

It is surprising, nevertheless, how often sets of company values do not specifically include anything related to learning or development. It is as if 'training' is accepted as something one has to do, without seeing its significance in actually facilitating or accelerating business goals. It is quite rare to find corporate statements of belief in any more detail other than paragraphs containing commitments 'to develop people to their full potential' or something similar.

A clear statement of beliefs will seriously aid the HRD director in creating an appropriate strategy. There are a number of options, which can be expressed as a polarised scale – from a minimalist approach to a dedicated learning organisation culture. A tool for testing this is shown in Figure 2.2. The tool asks people to say where they think the organisation *is* today, and where they think it *should* be. The latter help HRD determine their strategic position; the gaps indicate the priorities for change. If HRD issues have never been previously articulated, this tool can be used with a senior team. The HR or HRD director says 'My job is to spend HRD money wisely and in line with what the organisation wants – please help me do this by clarifying what you, the senior team, believe about people development.' A lively debate is likely to ensue – plus a clear sense of direction for HRD.

Figure 2.2 Strategic options for organisations in learning and development

Place a '*' for the desired position (as you feel would be best for your organisation) and an 'o' for the actual situation today. Join up the *'s and the o's. Which are the biggest gaps?

We act mostly on the basis that people are costs	We act mostly on the basis that people are assets
We are only interested in investing in high potentials	We believe in investing in the growth of all our employees
Our focus is on off-the-job training programmes	We believe continuous learning is a way of life
We hire and promote people already qualified for vacancies we have	We aim for internal promotion where possible and desirable
Managers decide what training is needed	We want all employees to take the prime ownership for their development
Vacancies are filled on an expediency basis	We believe in helping people manage their careers and linking this with our succession needs
We budget for the training we can afford	Investing in our people is a key competitive benchmark
We believe it is unwise to tell people views on their potential	It is better to be open and honest about the future
Learning by experimentation needs permission	Learning by experimentation is actively encouraged and mistakes are not blamed
We only do training that is for clear business benefit	We believe in developing people for their own benefit as well as ours

Some of the options, encapsulated in the tool in Figure 2.2, are as follows.

Do we regard people fundamentally as costs, or do we see them equally as assets?

'People are our most important asset' is a common enough statement, yet frequently lacks credibility as the people themselves see what comes first in priorities. The preoccupation with headcount that prevails in many organisations is driven by a cost mentality, even though it is a very crude measure of human resources expenditure. People *are* costs of course, and that cannot be ignored. However, unlike costs that are mere consumption, investment in them can increase their contribution and liberate potential. We started Chapter 1 with the place of people in building value for organisations.

Just as the homogenisation of people through 'headcount' is inappropriate when looking at costs, so it is true that people have very different asset values. Some

Figure 2.3 Human assets

Difficult to replace Low added value (eg long serving with extensive knowledge of systems and people; or having relatively low-level skills that are scarce) (*aim to motivate and retain*)	Difficult to replace High added value (eg leaders, core expertise, holders of key relationships, scarce specialists) (*retain at all costs*)
Easy to replace Low added value (eg people concerned with maintenance or admin activities) (*consider outsourcing*)	Easy to replace High added value (eg non-industry-specific specialists) (*aim for maximum productivity*)

employees are resources, easily replaceable and necessary to get tasks done; others are unique, high value added and fundamental to our core competence. One way to look at the spectrum of assets is on two dimensions – the ease of replacement and the ability to add value to stakeholders (see Figure 2.3). The latter is a function of both individual capability and the job people are currently doing. It is nothing to do with levels or grades. Losing somebody in the top right-hand category of Figure 2.3 should be considered as disastrous and expensive as losing a key customer.

The same policies and investment in learning would not apply to all – some require more attention and investment than others. An organisation wants to develop its human capital – but in an intelligent way.

APPLICATION

Think of some categories of staff in your organisation that would fit into each quartile of Figure 2.3. How does this relate to the normal ways to monitoring staff losses and would it be helpful to change that? What do you estimate as the cost of replacing individuals in the upper-right quadrant?

Implications for HRD strategy

In general, however, if the organisation has an 'asset' mentality, it will want to do the following:

- ensure employees are helped to regularly assess their potential

- ensure that employees are focusing on continual learning and development

- be concerned that it understands the talent it has; utilises and grows it effectively.

This will lead to strategies, policies and processes that recognise that people grow, and help them to do so. The strategy will be very different if the prevailing mentality is only 'costs', treating people as mere human *resources,* to be used for as long as they are useful.

When faced with the choice, most managements would aver that they recognise the asset value of people. The test comes when a short- or medium-term financial hurdle has to be crossed. I often ask audiences, "Who has senior management that *says* they believe people are their most important assets?" (nearly 100 per cent), and "Who has senior management who *act* as if they clearly believe it?" I am lucky to get 5–10 per cent saying yes to this second question. My own experience as an HR director, in situations where downsizing was needed, was that a little patience and some dedicated redeployment effort more often than not took care of keeping the assets as well as saving the cash drain of redundancy. Alas, few HR managers are bonused on cashflow!

APPLICATION

List some recent decisions in your organisation regarding the deployment and development of people. Do they indicate more of a 'costs' mentality or an 'assets' mentality?

Are we interested in investing only in those with potential for senior management or do we recognise potential in everybody?

Organisations have tended to distinguish between a training function covering all staff, and then special attention is given to *management* development. A wealth of assessment technology has been devoted to assessing potential for senior management, together with bibles of global leadership competencies. Of course, future senior management is a legitimate and serious concern; but this effort goes into at most 1 per cent or less of the available people. (They are perhaps best equipped to manage their own development anyway.) An alternative approach is this kind of statement:

❝ We believe everyone in this organisation has potential to grow, and shall make available the same systems and processes for people development to all. However, individuals will follow different development paths and some will require more help from the organisation than others. **❞**

Implications for HRD strategy

If we take the view expressed in the statement, we should provide tools and help for everyone to explore their potential, whether as management, technologist or other person with special skills. In Chapter 5 we look at different kinds of potential, and break out of the assumption that potential is only about 'onwards and ever upwards'.

Organisations need, for example, world-class specialists in their core competency areas just as much as capable managers.

This approach has practical implications for the design of individual development plans, for the provision of career planning help, and for the way we manage succession.

Do we focus on off-the-job training programmes or do we see continuous learning as a way of life?

Research shows that some 80 per cent of people's learning comes from experience, or work itself. Yet probably 80 per cent of the effort of most training departments is invested in off-the-job events and the administration surrounding them. If we have any ambition to be a learning organisation – and this is still a commonly found aspiration – we are going to see learning as continuous; both within and outside of the work situation.

Implications for HRD strategy

This has immense implications for HRD resourcing. If we have an objective of embedding learning as a way of life we are going to spend a lot of effort in working with units and teams helping them understand what it means to them. We shall work at individual, team and unit levels in creating a full understanding of learning styles, cycles and modes, enabling people to make good choices and to use the learning opportunities around them effectively. HRD will be constantly checking progress towards the desired culture and reviewing priorities accordingly.

Do we always seek qualified people who have been trained elsewhere, or offer opportunities to recruits and seek to major on internal promotion as a preference?

There is on the face of it quite a lot of financial sense in letting other people do the training necessary, to gain both qualifications and experience. For this reason, some organisations refuse to hire new graduates but look for those with two to four years work history. The alternative view is that loyalty and cultural empathy is created by 'growing your own'. Furthermore, the image of an attractive employer is enhanced by providing opportunities to gain initial or further qualifications.

It is still a popular strategy to pitch internal candidates against external ones for many vacancies, rather than looking outside only as a second resort. There is a case for both stances.

Implications for HRD strategy

The position taken here will affect graduate development programmes, further education policy, and career management processes.

Do managers decide what training is needed, or do individuals take primary ownership for their own development needs?

The tradition of organisations is one of hierarchy, where the 'father' and grandfather' approach is applied to the management of people. Because the managerial role is one of organising work and gaining results, it is naturally assumed that the 'boss' is the key person to advise on training, development or careers. The evidence is clear, however, that few managers do this well, despite training in feedback and coaching skills. Their priorities are with the tasks in hand. Many organisations persist in emphasising this managerial role, even going so far as to say the *primary* role that managers should have today is that of 'coach'. This is, in reality, rare – especially in middle and junior management, where the demands placed on them do not permit such a focus.

An alternative approach is to put the individual in the driving seat, and see the role of management as supportive rather than controlling.

Implications for HRD strategy

Where the organisation stands on this particular spectrum will have a profound effect on the HRD strategy and where it puts its emphasis on people-development skills. It will either train managers in carrying out their responsibility for needs diagnosis, feedback, preparing and managing learning plans, and coaching, or, if the organisation wishes to be more towards the personal ownership end of the spectrum, it will be investing a lot of time in helping people understand learning for themselves. This will include how to use the people around them effectively – and spending more time in coaching individuals to take care of their own needs.

Do we fill positions on an expediency basis, or prefer an approach that integrates individual career planning and the organisation's succession planning?

It has been common practice in recent years to tell employees that it is up to them to look after their careers, and to manage opportunities and vacancies expediently – without any sense of the long term. The downturn following 11 September 2001 and subsequent corporate scandals made companies pay more attention to longer-term planning. There is clearly a case for planning for 'continuity' of key positions; and at the same time for encouraging employees to plan ahead for their own careers.

Implications for HRD strategy

The issues here are how we help individuals do their own planning, do long-range planning for the organisation's resources, and build a process of dialogue between the two.

Is training and development budgeted as a cost to be minimised, or at a level that reflects its competitive importance?

Budgeting is often a strange art in organisations, a game to be played. Most budgeting systems fail to distinguish between expenditure that is actually an investment, and that which is a straight cost of doing business. 'Training' is likely to be a cost line of its own, with rules regulating what may be included and what may not. It will always be an imperfect measure of overall learning.

If our mentality is 'assets' oriented, we shall want to benchmark investment in people just as much as investment in product or service development. The alternative sees training as a discretionary spend, a candidate for cutbacks when times are hard despite a budget that may remain unspent.

What should we include in the 'investment' category? Not training that *has* to be done to keep the business going. However, spending on education, on potential development for the longer term, in supporting change and culture building – these all have a future payoff and could be justified as investment.

Implications for HRD strategy

This is clearly a matter of some importance to HRD. They should be well aware of how much activity and spend is in the two categories. Indeed, HRD might want to influence the thinking of top management regarding 'asset' investment. It will help considerably to have collected competitive data through benchmarking. I recall presenting such data to the board of my company at a time when budgets were under threat. Every competitor was spending more than we were and we were spending less per person than five years before. And yet we continually told the world we believed 'knowledge and skills made the difference'. I put it to the board that either we had better people to start with, or we spent our money to greater effect, or perhaps we were putting ourselves at a competitive disadvantage. Since our competitors included such companies as IBM, Hewlett Packard and Microsoft, it seemed the latter would be the

▶ Table 2.1 Openness vs secrecy in discussing potential

For openness	Against
■ Enables people to be active participants in their development	■ Fear of disappointment, conflict and demotivation *in some circumstances*
■ Encourages openness and honesty on both sides	■ Fear that the discussion will be difficult and will need a lot of preparatory work
■ Commitments made are more formal and more likely to be honoured	■ The knowledge that unforeseen *changes* may ruin our commitments and the built-up expectations, and end up in bitterness and disappointment
■ Judgements will be made on sounder evidence	■ All judgements about the future are subjective and therefore a dialogue based on them is inherently risky
■ Insecurity and suspicion about what is being written about people is removed	■ A lot of effort is needed to manage this well, and we do not have the resources
■ Manages expectations – helps people to make realistic plans	■ Managers are not skilled to handle these situations well
■ Mitigates frustration with 'lack of a route forward' and hence unwanted attrition	■ Managing resulting expectations is too difficult
■ Encourages consistency in operating the processes	■ The undesirability of distinctive 'labels' for individuals
■ Provides a motivational opportunity	■ Impacts on the team where one or more are 'set apart' from others
■ Legal requirements of Data Protection Acts	
■ Leads to 'holistic' and future-orientated personal development plans	

case. Units were instructed as a result to have all their training budgets at competitive levels.

Do we believe it is better to be open or cautious about discussing views of potential with people?

Many appraisal systems have a part for potential assessment that is never seen by the employee concerned. Some people are never told the extent to which they are, or are not, deemed capable to go further in the organisation. The arguments for the alternative approaches are given in Table 2.1.

The arguments for being secretive carry little or no weight in an organisation where we want people involved in their own development. Even without that, they are hard to justify as they lead to misunderstandings and demotivation.

Implications for HRD strategy

The impact here is on the design of 'dialogue processes' such as appraisal, and in training managers to 'manage' open discussions effectively.

Do we believe that people should be free to innovate and learn by experimentation?

Most managers will say 'of course'. But so many organisations actually have a culture of intolerance of mistakes, an inevitable result of free experimentation. So the question is not just one of encouragement but of the supportive culture surrounding the freedom to take risks in the interests of learning.

Implications for HRD strategy

This is a cultural and behavioural issue – HRD will need to ensure that managers know how to provide sensible freedoms and manage the learning that results.

Do we believe we do training only for clear business benefits, or do we offer training for personal development in its own right?

When challenged, most organisations and HRD departments will assert they do only what is in the interests of 'the business'. But this often makes some very tenuous assumptions about the business benefits of many programmes. The truth is that we do often pay for people to go on to training as a reward, and we may provide a range of personal development programmes that benefit the individual far more than the organisation. There is nothing wrong with this – it is part of the benefits from the organisation. But we should be clear and honest about the beneficiaries.

Answering this question will help us get the balance right – how many days are we prepared to invest in the employee per year for her or his own benefit?

Implications for HRD strategy

The answer to this would shape the portfolio of what is offered and the use of resources.

APPLICATION

Do the exercise in Figure 2.2 (page 42) for the organisation you are part of. Are there any areas where you think that top management might differ from your own judgement? How could you check that out?

It may well be that the answers to these questions are not clear at a senior team level. They should not be answered by HRD on behalf of the organisation, as they will inevitably be biased by the values of the function. It is a very useful intervention to give the tool in Figure 2.2 to the senior team, not individually, but when meeting together, and get them to thrash out what 'the organisation' believes. This will be immensely helpful to HRD, not only as a guide but also as an anchor of support.

A FEW WORDS ABOUT THE LEARNING ORGANISATION

Taken as a whole, the right-hand statements of Figure 2.2 could be said to describe some of the characteristics of a learning organisation to which many HRD functions would be personally committed. What is it that makes an organisation a 'learning organisation' – given that organisations do learn daily? The answer lies in the deliberate management of learning processes, and the distinctions were articulated by consultant and writer Bob Garratt in the first book on the subject, as follows:

- They (learning organisations) encourage people at all levels of the organisation to learn regularly and rigorously from their work.

- They have systems for capturing learning and moving it where it is needed.

- They value learning, and are able to continuously transform themselves.

The growing realisation that knowledge is a key asset, and the effectiveness of managing and sharing it a source of competitive advantage, have made more senior managers interested in creating a learning sharing culture. For this is what it is – a unifying concept for a culture of innovation, responsiveness, flexibility and change – these are desirable aspirations on the agenda of all managers.

If this is the case, it implies a very different mindset from that of the traditional training department. It is about learning permeating the organisation's culture; and about a widely distributed 'ownership' of continuous learning. Power is diffused from the training department as it becomes more consultative than controlling. Emphasis is placed on the process of learning rather than pre-programmed activities, even though they continue to serve a purpose.

A learning organisation is not just about good learning practice. It requires a supporting culture that *thinks* learning and values it seriously. Building such a culture requires a template, a description of the desired state against which progress can be measured. This requires some 'visioning' – describing 'what it would be like if this were a true learning organisation'. A framework such as that described by Burgoyne, Pedler and Boydell (1996) in their book *The Learning Company,* or by Mayo and Lank (1994) in their book *The Power of Learning,* can assist here. They have used models that define the contributing factors to a learning organisation (the latter based broadly on the popular European Business Excellence model), and posed questions to help teams assess where they are and where they might like to be.

APPLICATION

List 20 characteristics that would describe your organisation if it were a 'learning organisation'. How do you rate today on a scale of 1–10 on each? Which three to five areas would really benefit you if tackled deliberately as a change project over the coming year or two?

APPLICATION

Who in management sees it as part of his or her responsibility to manage the sharing of knowledge and experience? List any gaps and inefficiencies in this vital process and suggest some ways forward – such as who should be influenced, what systems and resources should be put in place, etc.

CORE COMPETENCES, OD STRATEGY, AND THE EXTERNAL ENVIRONMENT

The third of our general drivers is that of the core competences of the organisation. This is not the same as the values – which are generally aspirational. By 'core' we mean the fundamental expertise that enables the organisation to be in, and stay in, its field. Hopefully there are also some areas that distinguish a particular organisation positively from its competition, although these are not always so easy to find. It is these distinctive ones that make the difference, and if not clear it may be well worth choosing some to build.

The seminal work on business 'core' competencies is that of Hamel and Pralahad in *Competing for the Future* (1994). A 'core capability' requires that knowledge in it is continually updated, excellence is maintained, and all in the organisation who are affected by it will be evaluated for their expertise in it. The overall agenda for HRD must include continuous learning in the identified capabilities. In practice, the department may not actually manage many of the training courses and seminars, certainly of a technical nature, but it will be concerned to ensure they take place and are effective. Outsourcing these areas is likely to be inappropriate, since the organisation itself should have superior expertise as well as competitive advantage.

APPLICATION

What are the core competencies of your organisation? Are they generally explicit? What in your training portfolio is designed to support them?

It is common today to identify *behavioural* skills that are core, in addition to business, professional or technical know-how. These may be those identified to support the corporate *values,* and be applicable to every employee (as Richard Boyatsis of Case Western University observed in a personal statement, 'Competencies without values is like sex without love'), or – more commonly – they may be the desired characteristics of management, or leaders. As such, they will be chosen as those that will generate excellence and advantage for the particular business – although often competitors have very similar sets! HRD will be expected not only to help individuals assess their capability, but also to develop it. In 2004 Novell, the network company, identified five core competencies, listed below, 'that are characterized by behaviors we believe are vital to the success of every Novell employee'. These are very close to values, which should indeed form the core of any set of 'behavioural' competencies:

■ customer/client focus

- results orientation
- organisational impact
- interpersonal effectiveness
- self-management.

What about the OD strategy as a driver?

The case for integrating OD and people development in one function is very strong. They cannot be separated, unless HRD is a mere supplier of training courses.

Any OD strategy is going to need learning – at all levels. Major change programmes can be very demanding on the learning function. Without patient investment in mindset and attitude change, achieving the desired results will be hard work. HRD has to work at many levels of capability to support such change – facilitating workshops, providing appropriate knowledge inputs and helping people to learn across boundaries.

And external changes?

A useful tool here is the PESTLE analysis – the study of the political, economic, social, technological, legal and environmental factors. Particularly in the public sector, sociopolitical agendas require a response, in providing awareness or attitudinal training. There are strategic questions of support for governmental initiatives – such as the UK 'Investors in People' programme (see Chapter 8). The law is constantly changing – making its own demands for compliance (some of which may be for knowledge), but also requiring updates for managers and others from time to time. The UK has a strong social emphasis on qualifications and certification, and this leads to pressure from employees and trade unions.

Technology has brought about more change than anything else. Managers and employees constantly need technical training of various kinds, and technology has massively broadened the opportunities for delivering learning and sharing knowledge. HRD has to formulate its own strategy regarding the 'E-learning revolution', and we return to this in Chapter 6.

█ APPLICATION

Conduct a PESTLE analysis in respect of HRD and your organisation today. What factors and trends does it show up? Are you responding to them well enough at the moment?

PRINCIPLES, POPULATIONS, POLICIES, PROCESSES AND PROGRAMMES

The drivers above lead HRD into Part One of the HRD strategy – that which provides the overall people development framework and is semi-permanent. They enable us to:

- define and articulate our *principles* and beliefs about people development (see Chapter 8 for how to publicise these)

- subdivide the organisation into *populations* with common types of learning need

- define the *policies* to support those principles

- define a series of *programmes* to form a regular part of our portfolio

- define *processes* to support the involvement of all stakeholders in people development and make it work.

Populations

It is quite likely that not all policies and processes will apply to every employee in the same way. Certainly many learning programmes will be aimed at specific groups. It is helpful, therefore, to have a clear division of the organisation's human capital into 'populations' for each of which we may have a substrategy.

A typical breakdown of an organisation might look like Figure 2.4. These are groups with common types of learning needs, and we may have substrategies for each of these.

Figure 2.4 Dividing an organisation into populations with common learning needs

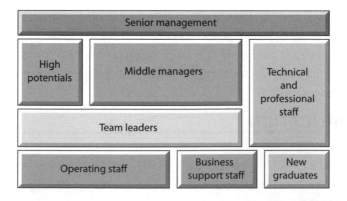

APPLICATION

Draw up the key subgroupings of people in your organisation who have common development needs. Do you have specific strategies for each?

Policies

Policies are a practical expression of our beliefs. They provide guidance to managers and employees in deciding courses of action. They represent *continuing* activities, and in this way are distinct from strategies, which represent directional choices. Compared to general HR, there are a limited number of policy areas in HRD. However, they will be less administrative and more strategic in their connection to the direction, values and beliefs of the organisation.

The test of a good policy is that managers understand clearly what to do without seeking further help. Having said that, policies that give discretion to the manager might please some managers but irritate others, who may like absolutely clear guidance.

We look first at some of the strategic choices in policy formulation and then at some specific areas where policies are needed.

How detailed and prescriptive should policies be?

Principles and beliefs should be universal – they should be formulated so that they are independent of local laws, customs and cultures. However, the practical application of those beliefs may, and often should, vary.

Organisations provide different degrees of freedom to their operations in how principles are applied. A spectrum runs from 'we lay down principles only and leave interpretation to the units' to 'we research and define best practice in HQ and expect all our units to adopt it'. Many American organisations adopt the latter view and dictate *procedures* as well as the general policies; British companies tend to do this less. Table 2.2 shows an example of decreasing degrees of freedom in the use of appraisal systems:

There is no right answer, of course – it depends on the kind of culture the organisation wants and the issue. ICL, the computer company, in re-evaluating its cultural framework after several mergers, produced a booklet called *The Management Framework* which aimed to lay down the *minimum* set of policies that would be universal. For HR there were 10, each described in one sentence, and in total there were about 30. This was a reaction to a formerly heavy hand from the centre, and also a genuine belief at that time

▶ Table 2.2 Degrees of freedom in appraisal systems

■ It is a principle in our organisation that every employee should have a regular formal discussion regarding their performance and development.
■ It is our policy that each unit should develop a performance appraisal system based on performance objectives, evaluate overall performance with a rating system, and discuss performance improvement and career development.
■ All local appraisal systems must utilise the global performance rating system, will appraise against the company's values and universal competency framework, and will be completed by the end of March annually.
■ All appraisals will conform to the Corporate Guidelines, and use Form XXXX, issue YY, translated as necessary to local language.

that 'empowerment within policy and strategic guidelines' was a better way to manage and motivate people.

One key question to ask is: For whose benefit is this policy? If it is for the benefit of local employees then the more localised the application probably the more useful it will be. If, however, it is for the benefit of the organisation itself, then more consistency in application is needed. With today's centralised shared services, often globally, there is a great desire to have common approaches throughout, but it is still important to be sure that the expected benefits are being perceived locally when this is done. Examples of HRD policy areas are given in Table 2.3.

APPLICATION

What 'global' policies exist in your organisation? Who primarily benefits from them? Do you feel the balance between global and local is right?

▶ Table 2.3 Global/local policies

Tends to be more localised	Tends to be more globalised
Technical training	'Core competence' training
Education and qualifications	Graduate development
'Soft' skills training	Management development
Capability assessment	Succession planning
Trainee schemes	Potential classification

When we have mergers, acquisitions and alliances, how critical is it to move to common policies?

This is an exciting area for HR and HRD, and absorbs an immense amount of time and resources. There is a fundamental policy decision, which is about (a) convergence and (b) its speed. Many companies exhibit an obsessive haste to create neatness out of disorder – common policies and approaches as soon as possible. Others value the diversity of experience that is available and seek to learn from it before creating compromise or imposing unilateral approaches.

There is much merit in taking the time to appreciate where talent, knowledge and wisdom lie in any new partner and seeing that as important a part of the relationship as any financial or market share gain. HRD would expect to play a significant role in this. *Synergy*, a word that analysts have come to see as potential cost cuts, should be about the fusion of intellectual capital and capability. What could be a more strategic role for the HRD director? Fusing appraisal systems can wait!

To what extent should discretion be given to individual managers?

This is always a dilemma. Fairness means consistency of treatment to many people. But everyone is different; what matters to one may not be the same as to another, and our culture may be one of empowerment – so we do not want policy guidelines that remove managerial judgement and are 'one size fits all'. We should start from the principle that we want to give discretion wherever possible – and give detailed guidance only where different interpretations will give *significant* difficulty.

How much help shall we offer to employees for further education?

We have to decide:

- what kinds of further education we shall support, either because it is relevant to our business or in accordance with a policy of encouraging continual learning and development for employees
- whether we shall distinguish in terms of assistance between the two categories
- what we shall offer in terms of time and money
- what level of discretion we shall give to local managers.

'Accreditation' refers to certificates of achievement following a defined course approved by an authoritative external body. Sometimes a necessary passport to a specialist career or to client acceptance, it is also one of the routes to employability. This arena covers, in the UK:

- *Professional qualification,* eg accountancy, personnel, purchasing or chartered engineer. As a means of attracting staff, help may be promised towards the appropriate qualification – although the value placed on these attainments is variable. Since many of the people seeking help are young, most organisations will help employees with both time and money. (It is common to pay 50 per cent of fees up front and 50 per cent on successful completion.) Membership fees will normally be paid for students, but not necessarily after qualification.

- *Business qualifications* used to embrace certificates such as the DMS (Diploma of Management Studies) and others, but today strongly focus on the MBA. MBAs come in many shapes and sizes, from the concentrated in-depth two-year full-time course, to the part-time, correspondence or virtual (via the Internet) degree. Most organisations (with exceptions in the major consulting firms) would not sponsor full-time MBAs because they know that the salary expectations will rise by 30–50 per cent (for a prestigious school), and they cannot cope with this internally. They will, however, fund part-time courses – totally or partially, often stipulating that a half of the reimbursement is dependent on successful completion.

- *National Vocational Qualifications (NVQs)* is another area where a policy will be needed. The choices concern which areas should be supported by the organisation and to what level, and how much they should be customised. Scottish and Newcastle Breweries is one company that has invested an immense amount of effort to customise NVQs for pub management, and found a direct relationship between pub success, employee motivation and the level of qualifications obtained by the staff. Many organisations, however, are put off by the bureaucracy and complexity that can be involved. For an excellent summary of NVQs see Rosemary Harrison's book *Learning and Development* (2002).

To what extent shall we fund personal development?

If we have a policy to support staff by encouraging them to manage their own development and careers, we must make choices as to what level of support can be provided. Some of the questions to be answered include:

- Physical learning resource centres have been supplemented or overtaken by e-resources, but how much shall we make available to employees? How broad ranging will be the offerings – will they go beyond work-relevant learning? Shall we allow access in 'normal' working hours?

- Shall we provide career development workshops or counselling? To what extent will they be voluntary? Will people be left to themselves afterwards or shall we provide mentoring or further support?

- Shall we fund nonbusiness-related personal development? Should this be done by an allocated sum of money to each individual (as, for example, in Bodyshop), or provide a 'pot' for allocation/negotiation by managers? Shall we place any boundaries on what will be funded?

One way to encourage personal development is to offer 'prizes' or 'bonuses' for job-related achievements which are learning related. Thus, a 'sum of money to be spent on books or a course' may be offered, or a visit to another part of the organisation, or some opportunity linked with customers or suppliers.

APPLICATION

Brainstorm with some colleagues how you might introduce new ways of encouraging personal development through prizes and incentives. How would they be introduced and would there be any barriers to be overcome?

Do we want a policy on mentoring and external coaching?

The policy on mentoring in the organisation may vary from nothing at all, to the open provision of trained mentors to anyone who would like one. Generally this is one area not available to all our populations. In the turbulence of organisations today the anchoring point of an experienced person who is prepared to counsel and care seems very desirable. The provision and the supply of external coaches has grown exponentially. Although much of their work is supporting development needs arising from 360° feedback analysis, much is also what would be better described as general mentoring.

Since these activities are confidential between mentor/coach and the employee, the organisation itself may see little actual benefit. Such provisions should be seen as a supplement to our internal framework of people development and not as a substitute.

Questions for HRD to answer are:

- For whom should we offer this benefit?
- How consistent will this be with our stated beliefs on people development?
- To what extent shall we train mentors and mentees?
- Will taking up the benefit be voluntary?
- How shall we manage the 'matching' process?
- What ongoing support shall we provide for mentors?
- To whom shall we offer *external* mentors and how will this be managed?

APPLICATION

For whom does your organisation offer mentoring at the present time? What is the rationale in choosing them and not others? How does your policy here reflect your general beliefs on people development?

When people move up (or across) the organisation, do we want any 'rites of passage'?

Rituals may accompany the transition from one population to another – in the form of selection and assessment processes, and prescribed learning programmes. These may be triggered by a new level of management responsibility, or be modules of core competence training. Over time, managers and staff may be expected to collect a 'portfolio' of personal skills. Competence frameworks often define requirements by organisational levels.

Many courses become enshrined in the culture, and bestow their own status. There is always a need for constantly updating the relevance of these courses, and in fact a great amount of HRD spend may be devoted to them. However, the *content* of the courses may be less important than the benefits of creating networks of people who can benefit from each other's experience across the organisation.

These events may be external – some well-known companies routinely send executives at a certain point in their careers for the three-month course in Harvard, or a senior executive programme elsewhere. Others partner with a school to provide, for example, an executive MBA, or regular customised courses that people are expected to attend.

APPLICATION

List all the established 'rites of passage' in your organisation. For each, how long have they been in existence? What measures are used to assess their benefit currently to the organisation? Are they the right measures and what do they tell us? Does this analysis provide any indicators for change?

How will equal opportunity and diversity principles be applied in HRD?

Every organisation today will have some statement of equal opportunity and/or diversity. It may be a bland nondiscriminating statement, or be more specific – even positively discriminating. Public sector organisations like to aim for an organisational distribution of race, gender, etc that reflects the community in which they work. Whilst this is clearly a desirable aim, it is frequently difficult to achieve.

The more subtle issues here are not concerned with appointments and statistics. The danger of all statistics and averages is in the assumption that people have equal values and motivations about progression. True equal opportunity may mean valuing individual diversity and being flexible in the way we meet individual needs and life balance requirements. Equal opportunity for *learning* would be a concern for the HRD director – including practical policies regarding continuous learning for those unable to have full-time contracts, or on maternity leave.

What about the development of noncore staff

Organisations today are far less homogeneous than before, when almost everybody was on a defined contract, either full- or part-time, together with all the benefits of contractual employment. So the 'core' of contracted employees is complemented by what Americans call 'contingent workers' – temporary skills, regular contractors, interim managers, outsourcing partners, etc. Free of the liabilities associated with contracts, where does this leave employers in respect of development?

Again we have two polarities of choice:

- 'Contracted resources have to look after their own skills development'
- 'All our resources need to be at the highest level of competence. We have a part to play in ensuring that.'

There are many answers here, and many dependencies. Here are some factors to take into account:

- the *potential* value added of the resource
- the need for team co-ordination and learning together, core and others
- the amount of time committed to the organisation by the resource
- whether the resource is involved in something that is strategically a priority
- the individual's opportunity for self-development.

The nature of the help given may include:

- invitations to team learning events
- technical updates
- 'bonuses' as learning credits to be used on company courses
- free books and multimedia
- access to e-learning resources.

APPLICATION

What kinds of noncore resources do you employ in your organisation? List for each the approach to their development that is adopted, and the resource's alternative means of personal growth. How might greater benefit accrue to your organisation by changing the levels of provision?

At one extreme might be the software programmer who works on a team for two years. He or she is indistinguishable from other contractors except in terms of contract, pay rate and benefits. As far as work and contribution is concerned, his or hers is as important as any other member of the team. So one would expect participation in everything the team learns, and in all its training. If such a person has an appraisal, however, it will probably focus on performance standards and short-term training needs rather than on longer-term development.

Another situation might be the consultant who comes in to do occasional training courses in their areas of specific expertise. A regular resource, she or he might need to be kept in touch with organisational developments, progress and strategies – and in addition be involved in the sharing of learning that takes place in the group. In contrast, the temporary secretary who comes in for four weeks from an agency may find that she or he has to look after their own skill development – unless the agency provides ongoing training itself.

Processes and tools

A key part of our HRD strategy will be a framework of processes that support our principles and beliefs in people development. Depending on those principles, we shall be considering processes such as the following:

- performance and development reviews
- personal development plans
- learning needs analysis
- induction
- knowledge management
- development needs assessment
- feedback processes
- role and personal profiling.

These are discussed in Chapter 4. HRD will want to continually monitor their effectiveness, so that those who should benefit from them see them as valuable and not as a mere routine to be gone through.

In career and continuity management (Chapter 5) we have:

■ vacancy management

■ succession planning

■ resource planning

■ organisational mapping

■ personal career planning.

Devolved organisations, as are common today, may develop their own HRD strategies. However, in the area of career and continuity one would expect unified cross-sector, cross-region policies and processes. After all, one of the benefits of an organisation with many parts should be to have the benefit of knowledge and talent sharing.

We shall also deploy a number of professional tools that support these processes, such as:

■ capability frameworks

■ potential classification

■ assessment tools.

Our strategy will define the processes we want to have. The supporting plans will detail those we need to introduce, and also those we want to 're-engineer' because they are not as effective as we would like.

Programmes

The core of HRD's portfolio will be a set of learning programmes supporting the five drivers discussed at the beginning of this chapter. (Table 2.4 shows an example.) These will be programmes run regularly for as long as needed to support the 'umbrella strategy'. We shell add to them programmes that support current business needs, as discussed in the next chapter.

▸ Table 2.4 Examples of programmes for supporting the 'umbrella' strategy

Strategic driver	Programmes
Mission, vision, values, objectives	■ induction ■ graduate development programme ■ 'values in action' workshops ■ large contract negotiations
People management beliefs	■ managing your learning ■ giving and receiving feedback ■ coaching skills
Core competences	■ technical and business modules ■ competency training ■ team leadership
OD strategy	■ supporting workshops ■ change management ■ knowledge exchange and utilisation
External influences	■ sexual harassment training ■ employment law ■ office technology

■ IN BRIEF

■ Part One of our HRD strategy is to support the ongoing organisation in terms of what it is and where it wants to go. This means examining the mission, vision and values and asking how we support them with learning. We also need to study the organisational development strategy, if there is one, and external factors affecting people development.

■ A key part of this umbrella strategy is the set of principles the organisation wishes to hold in respect of people development. These may or may not have been articulated. Senior management should be involved in defining them – this then gives an invaluable steer to HRD choices.

■ We shall support the drivers of this longer-term strategy through appropriate policies, and ongoing programmes for particular groups of people. 'Principles' should be common everywhere and should guide the policies. But the application of these may vary with national situations, with different groups of employees, and with historical situations arising from, for example, mergers. Our willingness to tolerate diversity will be a reflection of our general culture.

- It is helpful to divide the organisation into 'populations' with common learning needs, for whom we shall have particular plans and programmes.

- Processes for people development that involve employees are vital, and they need to have credibility and be seen to add value rather than waste time and be a mere routine to be gone through. Good professional tools and diagnostics can help this credibility.

REFERENCES AND FURTHER READING

BURGOYNE J., PEDLER M. and BOYDELL T. (1996) *The Learning Company*. Maidenhead, McGraw Hill.

DAVIDSON H. (2002) *Committed Enterprise: How to make values and visions work*. Butterworth Heinemann.

GARRATT B. (2002) *The Learning Organisation: Developing democracy at work*. HarperCollins.

GRATTON L. (2000) *Living Strategy*. FT/Prentice Hall.

HAMEL G. and PRALAHAD C.K. (1989) 'Strategic intent'. *Harvard Business Review*, May–June.

HAMEL G. and PRALAHAD C.K. (1994) *Competing for the Future*. Cambridge, Mass, Harvard Press.

HARRISON R. (2002) *Learning and Development*. 3rd edn. London, CIPD.

LONGWORTH N. and DAVIES W.K. (1996) *Lifeling Learning*. Routledge Falmer.

MAYO A.J. and LANK E. (1994) *The Power of Learning*. London, IPD.

MUMFORD A. (1997) *Management Development: Strategies for action*. London, IPD.

PORRAS J.I. and COLLINS J.C. (1994) *Built to Last*. New York, Harpers Press.

PROKESCH S. and BROWNE J. (1997) 'Unleashing the Power of Learning: An interview with John Browne'. *Harvard Business Review*, September.

SEMLER R. (1994) *Maverick*. London, Arrow.

SENGE P. (1990) *The Fifth Discipline*. New York, Doubleday.

http://www.unitedmedia.com/comics/dilbert/career/bin/ms2.cgi

3 ■ SUPPORTING TODAY'S PRIORITIES

We have spent some time considering the 'general' drivers of strategy, which provide the umbrella for our activities but also have to be continually supported through learning. We now need to ask how HRD will support the *current* business goals and operations. This chapter looks at two sets of drivers that need to be considered – first those that are about moving the organisation *forward* and needing learning support, and second those that are *remedial* in the sense of helping to solve a problem or correct a deficiency. More often than not, such problems have their causes in a lack of capability at some level.

We introduce a general tool for deriving learning goals from business goals – the 'eight-step method' – and provide examples of its use in practice.

Objectives and problems change from year to year so there is a need for a disciplined process of keeping in touch with what is happening, and certainly an alignment with the objective setting cycle. The business-aware HRD director will keep eyes and ears open, and be a regular student of ongoing business information.

DERIVING LEARNING GOALS FROM BUSINESS GOALS

We can easily assent to the role of HRD in 'supporting the business'. The question is 'how?' It's not just a question of showing how what we do has business benefit. It is about starting with the business itself and using a disciplined methodology. We cannot escape from the imperative of having a solid understanding of business in general, and a genuine interest (ideally plus experience) in the challenges of the particular organisation to which we belong. So the question is: How do we make the critical link between a business driver and the learning goals that will support it?

▶ **Table 3.1   Building learning goals from business goals – in eight steps**

Table 3.1 describes a series of eight steps that can be used for deriving learning objectives from all the drivers – from the umbrella factors discussed in the last chapter, as well as current goals and issues.

Business goals and strategies exist at different levels. They may be at a *corporate* level – for the organisation as a whole. These will be high-level goals, and will be cascaded or sometimes repeated at *divisional* level. *Departments* and *teams* will have their own sets of targets, many of which will not relate directly to corporate strategies but reflect the ongoing role they have in the organisation. Finally, *individual managers* have their sets of objectives to achieve. The latter two sets will typically be dominated by a one-year timescale, whereas the first two will be a mix of long- and short-term goals. The achievement of goals at all levels is likely to involve *change*, and the task of the HRD professional is to understand where *changes in capability* – at any level – will assist or even accelerate the achievement of business goals. Not all HRD managers will have access to all the levels of business goals – however, the questions below are designed to assist this process at any level.

The series of logical steps here can equally be applied to solving *performance problems*, where instead of 'milestones to be achieved' it is *measurable performance gaps* that need to be closed.

1 For any given goal, what are the *milestones*, if any, towards its achievement?	Without milestones, many strategies and goals can serve as little more than wish-lists or dreams, and their chance of being achieved will be low. Effort and resources must be dedicated, and that requires progress to the goal to be inbuilt into the action plans of individuals. A milestone is simply a *measurable statement* of what we want to have achieved *at the end of* a planning period.
2 How will this milestone be achieved or – if it is a performance problem – the performance gap be closed? What are the *influencing factors* that need to be managed to ensure success?	Milestones are not achieved through the mere passing of time. They require action, and this critical step is about looking at the causal influences that affect achievement one way or another. We can identify positive forces (both external and internal) that should be strengthened, and negative ones that can be reduced or eliminated, and there may be completely new initiatives to be taken.

▶ Table 3.1 – continued

3	Who (the whole organisation, subgroups and/or individuals) is involved in causing change?	It is people who design and implement processes, and are involved in every aspect of change. This step identifies all those who have some responsibility for and/or involvement in the factors outlined in the previous step.
4	What components of their capability (skills, knowledge, personal capabilities, experience, networks, values and attitudes) drive the factors above, and what is the level we need?	It is highly likely that achieving the milestone will be dependent on a *new* level of capability in individuals and/or groups. We may need change in the whole organisation in some cases. We need to define the level(s) of capability needed for success. Appropriate and balanced 'competency frameworks' can assist us considerably.
5	Do we need any diagnostic tools to determine the level of that capability?	There will be situations where the present level of capability may not be at all clear. For example, we may have a strategic goal to 'create a more open blame-free learning culture'. We may have an intuitive feel of how it is today, but in order to help the change some clearer analysis is going to help us. So we may need to create some measuring instruments that can assess 'gaps' and the progress in closing them.
6	What, therefore, are the *learning objectives* that need to be set in order to close the learning gaps we have identified?	This is the vital step that will guide us in choosing the most effective routes. Objectives should follow the 'SMART' acronym – specific, measurable, achievable, relevant and time related.
7	How sure are we that the individuals concerned have the capability to make the changes?	This is a sensitive area, and the truth is that we may not be sure at all. More often than not, we give people the benefit of the doubt and consequently can waste time and money and frustrate people as they realise their inability to cope. Wherever possible, we should assess 'aptitude' for the change in capability needed.
8	Do we have the time to make the capability changes, or should we recruit or subcontract for them?	Whether the aptitude is there or not, it could still be the case that some changes will take a long time to achieve, especially if they are attitude or experience objectives. Our milestone may be achieved faster by buying in the capability we need – although this may have undesirable side effects and the answer might be to revisit the milestone itself.

The 'eight-step method'

This 'eight-step method' has the following features:

- It focuses on the importance of *quantification* of goals or performance gaps.

- It involves understanding the *business drivers* that affect the desired end state, both positively and negatively.

- It embraces *all* those who influence those drivers and leads us to specific individuals or groups who are critical in achieving the goal.

- It encourages the clear definition of capability levels as learning goals, and the use of appropriate measuring instruments for them.

- It does not assume there is a training solution.

- It does not assume that everyone can achieve the desired level of capability.

In contrast, below is a parody of an approach that is all too common, creating an illusion of being business linked but containing wild assumptive leaps from step to step:

❝ We have a problem of falling sales and market share =
Management is clearly not doing a good job =
We need better managers and leaders =
We'd better do some leadership training =
We'll use a competency framework for 360° assessment =
We'll design a programme around the major gaps we find. **❞**

This is the kind of spurious cause and effect chain thinking that HRD people may be guilty of, as it leads them into their comfort zones. A true business analysis may well have led us to identify problems with sale force competence or retention, new product innovation, noncompetitive cost structures, quality problems, and so on.

Using the eight steps in practice

The practical process for applying the method would entail the following:

- The Learning Consultant would prepare for the discussion by finding out as much as is possible about the business unit to be studied, and by having to hand any descriptions of capability that are relevant, or any appropriate diagnostic tools.

- He or she would prepare some working sheets in advance (examples are shown in Tables 3.2–3.5).

- The consultant either leads a structured discussion with representatives of the unit concerned, or has an interview with the manager of the unit.

- Step 2 will yield a number of factors that will influence the goal, working for or against. Some will be more significant than others. Using a format such as that used in Table 3.2 to list the influences, they need prioritising. One way is to distribute 100 percentage points between the factors.

■ Step 3 focuses on the critical factors and should identify both key individuals, such as particular managers, as well as groups of staff. The worksheet used in Table 3.3 can be used to do this, and also for Steps 4 and 5. Each person or group of people should be categorised as 'critical', 'important' or 'helpful'.

■ It may be necessary to create some diagnostics or measures if no suitable ones are available. Typically this will be in the form of levels of capability. Many competency frameworks are confined to personal behaviours and are not comprehensive enough for our needs – which are most likely to include aspects of know-how, experiences or contacts. Specifically defining the level we need will provide the learning objective.

■ Step 6 may take some time, as the diagnostics are applied to relevant groups and individuals in order to determine capability gaps. Some self- and peer assessment may be needed in addition to managerial judgement.

■ We do Steps 7 and 8, and on the assumption we want to go ahead we then check on any practical constraints of time and money before moving into selecting the best way of achieving the learning goals.

EXAMPLE 1

The 'eight-step' method is best applied using worksheets. The first example in Table 3.2 is for one of the organisational business drivers.

Let us suppose we have a long-term strategic goal as follows:

> ❝ To be recognised as the most innovative company in our business sector with greater than 15 per cent market share in every one of our geographic markets. ❞

There are actually two separate visionary goals here – one to be the *most innovative*, and the other about *market share*. They are connected of course, but so is everything in business!

In Step 1 we need to have some measure for 'innovation'. What do we mean by 'most innovative'? How will it be measured? Are we talking products, marketing or organisation? Whom shall we compare against, and are the data available? How far behind are we now (if at all)? What is our catch-up target for the next year?

▶ Table 3.2 Example 1: Steps 1 and 2 – factors of influence

Business driver:	To be the most innovative company in our industry sector.		
Quantified goal	**Current state**	**Factors influencing the goal achievement**	**Relative importance of impact**
1. Percentage of sales attributable to products introduced in past three years – target 25 per cent	Currently 17 per cent – best in sector is 22 per cent	▪ Understanding of the market needs by R&D ▪ Culture of innovation in R&D ▪ Percentage of ideas commercially viable ▪ Time to market ▪ Rewards that encourage innovation	40 15 20 20 5
2. Percentage of savings due to new or re-engineered processes p.a. Target 5 per cent	Best in sector not known Currently 2.2 per cent	▪ Rewards that encourage innovation ▪ Lack of fear and positive attitude to change ▪ Time and encouragement to experiment	20 25 55

Perhaps the most commonly used is the percentage of sales that comes from products/services introduced in, say, the past three years (the figure depends on the nature of the business). So, if our planning period is 12–18 months ahead, how much of the total gap should we target to close in that time? We can also look at internal innovation through cost savings from process change.

Step 2 requires consultancy skills and reasonable business knowledge to probe with the right questions. Sometimes we shall find line managers have not thought this through for themselves and so we need to question sensitively. In this case a number of influences are identified and 100 points split between them.

The second worksheet, in Table 3.3, focuses on the people and their capability. We have a mixture of groups and one key individual. This example is not necessarily complete – there will be more relevant capabilities than shown. It suggests we have 'diagnostics' – in this case capability definitions – for all but the salespeople. The right-hand column in Table 3.3 will lead us to the specification of the learning goals.

▷ Table 3.3 Example 1: Steps 3, 4 and 5 – people and their capability

Business driver:	To be the most innovative company in our industry sector.			
Key success factor:	Understanding of the market by R&D.			
Key people	Level of influence	Capability needed	Diag-nostic?	Is there a gap? How critical?
Sales-people	C	■ Ability to understand customer business and think of products/services that would help them	no	Only about 15 per cent of salespeople are good at this, leaving wide gaps in coverage. This is a critical problem
Sales managers	I	■ Providing time and encouragement to salespeople to listen to customers	yes	SMs continually push for sales results and so this is not done well
R&D director	C	■ Flexibility in project programming ■ Understanding of what will be commercial ■ Motivating people to change projects	yes	He is at an acceptable level on scheduling and flexibility but needs to be better on commercial understanding. This is critical; too many projects fail in the market
R&D teams	C	■ Listening to salespeople ■ Conducting customer focus groups themselves ■ Changing development priorities quickly	yes	About 25 per cent of R&D people really market oriented – others are techies. This is a serious problem

C= critical; I = important; H=helpful.

We can see immediately that we shall generate a number of separate 'paths' to follow, and a particular driver may have several worksheets.

APPLICATION

Try applying the eight-step method to the mission, vision and one or two value statements that you have in your organisation. You will need to follow one path at a time. (It will help to create your own worksheets.) Does the exercise reveal any gaps that either HRD or the line management are not addressing?

PROACTIVE GOALS

Managers have a range of objectives for the year: some are about achieving the current quantitative goals; others about new initiatives or plans for change and improvement.

Our model in Figure 1.6 had three kinds of proactive drivers:

- business strategies and goals
- organisational and human resource plans
- change initiatives.

Business strategies and goals

Every manager has targets to achieve, and usually some change projects to manage. Goals, targets and objectives are typically financial, market related, growth related, even cultural or – occasionally – people related. We may interact with them at corporate, divisional, departmental or individual levels. The question for HRD is where and how they should make connections to these goals in order to apply methodologies such as the 'eight steps' described above.

Are financial goals the concern of HRD? Very much so! It is only people who achieve goals, and they do not usually do so by just working harder. Achieving a growth objective, for example, may involve more efficient use of systems, better retention of staff, new sales techniques, improved negotiation, etc – growth does not just happen naturally. The experienced HRD director will develop an understanding of these factors and know what the possible implications for people and their capability are.

Many goals will be interdependent and it may not be necessary or feasible to take every one individually, but to see them as part of a whole. We shall probably not have the time and resources to systematically apply our consultant method universally, and so we may need to seek guidance from managers as to which are the priorities and which will rely *most* on better people capability.

Organisational and human resource plans

Organisational *change* may be part of a phased long-term OD strategy, but more often is a series of initiatives from HQ that consume an immense amount of time and energy. New CEOs – whether from inside, outside or the result of a merger – seem to gravitate immediately towards restructuring – asking, not *should* I reorganise, but *how* shall I do it? The top team may be advised by consultants that they would be more successful with a new model; and mergers and alliances almost always result in organisational upheaval. Market and technology changes force organisational change; and the constant pressure on costs causes widespread delayering and 'rightsizing'. It is positive to be flexible and adaptive; however, the *cost* of broken teams, relationships and new learning curves is rarely taken into account in the justifications for change.

Traditional organisation planning focuses first on the *positions* to be filled, and then on the people to fill them. Occasionally it starts the other way round – how can we use the talent we have? The former forces greater learning as people grow into new roles – although a combination of both approaches makes most sense.

When it happens, it immediately triggers questions in the mind of the HRD manager, who preferably should be involved at the planning stage. These would include:

- *Does this change require a significant capability shift for groups of people to make it successful?* An example is a shift to a matrix organisation. It is more often than not *after* the event we find out that people do not know how to work in such an environment; that they do not understand the cultures involved in their new responsibilities, or the market needs. Time and again, multinationals give home-based managers responsibility for countries about which they know nothing. HRD should be experienced enough to discuss the competencies needed objectively and check who has a learning need. People are sadly too impatient to get on with the new roles, and in so doing cost their organisation unnecessary pain and money.

- *Does this change require significant learning curves for certain individuals?* Taking out layers in an organisation inevitably increases the accountability of those people below the vanished rank. Especially if relatively senior, they may be reluctant to admit that they are in new waters, and prefer to learn as they go. This is rarely efficient, and can be costly. HRD needs to adopt a counselling mode, with knowledge of the requirements of the roles, and the ability to help the person assess their capability realistically. This is also important with international appointments – where ignorance of managing in different cultures can prove disastrous.

■ *Does the change set up new boundaries and render obsolete existing mechanisms for exchange of knowledge and networking?* How will knowledge be managed and transferred freely in the new structure? Will new systems and networking opportunities be needed? This should be a part of the planning and an area of expertise on which HRD can advise.

APPLICATION

List some problems you are aware of from recent reorganisations and try to cost those problems, if only approximately. How could more 'people capability planning' beforehand have prevented the problems, and at what cost?

Human resource planning is often neglected in the turbulence of corporate change, and some may feel it has little point to it. It is not the same as headcount control, which is a convenient and crude, if flawed, means of controlling people costs. It does include determining the *numbers* and *capability* of staff needed, but also analysing *human resource flows* is a vital guide to the planning of strategic *development*.

The business plan drives a set of numbers, including – let us say – 'a people inventory plan'. One reason headcount alone is unhelpful is that it assumes the same level of capability and contribution from each 'head'. The plan should detail the numbers of employees of different skills levels needed to deliver the financial, market share and service-level goals. These numbers may be determined in various ways:

■ *By deriving an affordable 'headcount' number from financial planning.* This is a very rough and ready calculator, and takes no account of the different costs and added value from different groups and skill levels. It is quite inadequate for strategic capability planning.

■ *Job category/skill numbers by productivity.* More sophisticated, this looks at the implications of improving a productivity ratio from its existing level rather than from just a cost parameter.

■ *Ratio planning.* For indirect staff categories not connected with a front-line delivery, this is similar to the previous method, for example by relating support levels to numbers of front-line staff.

■ *Zero-based budgeting.* Starting from an imaginary 'greenfield', what should we need, given no history? This method involves benchmarking 'best practice', and is always useful to do. It rarely gives all the answers on its own, as organisations always have the current reality as a base.

- *Process re-engineering.* This is similar to the zero base, but examines all the processes for inefficiencies and improvements *first*.

- *'Added value' analysis.* This looks at where and how much added value is being added to the organisation's goals by each function in *cost terms* and ensures resources are being utilised in the high added value areas.

- *Expertise planning.* This is about having the right people with the right skills at the right time. Taking the average *numbers* per staff category, we then break this down into the levels of expertise needed – so many with the top level, so many with at least some of the expertise. The outputs will be of great interest to HRD. We compare:

Required $(Q_1 \times E_m) + (Q_2 \times E_{(<m)})$ and Current $\Sigma(Q \times E)$

where Q = number of people, and $E_m / E_{(<m)}$ = Expertise at top level (m) and other levels (<m). We can then create a capability planning matrix which takes each critical capability and assesses how many more 'person years' we need of it.

Change initiatives

Today, change programmes are ubiquitous and often so numerous that they become a burden on management. Most managers are conscious of several in which they are expected to play their part, in addition to their main accountabilities. It may be quality or customer related, process engineering, organisational restructuring, new systems, supply chain efficiency, alliances – the list is extensive. *Managing* change is a key preoccupation, and a source of much revenue to 'change consultants'. The basic guidelines for being effective should by now be well understood; unfortunately, applying them all in conditions of insecurity and turbulence proves more difficult. Change initiatives invariably require training support, both in managing the *process* of change and in creating new levels of capability in individuals and teams. An established change methodology would include a step of evaluating new capability needs, and should include looking at all the stakeholders in a change, not just the obvious people affected.

Many organisations have a stated 'value' about being adaptable to change, in which case learning what this means would be a regular programme. The 'eight-step' methodology applies here equally well.

APPLICATION

List the major change initiatives current in your organisation. When and how did HRD get involved in each implementation? Could you see ways in which a different level of involvement could help the initiative?

REMEDIAL DRIVERS

Our model suggested four categories of this kind of driver:

- operational issues
- individual needs
- team needs
- external changes.

Being responsive to a cry for help comes naturally to most HRD departments, but to do so effectively requires considerable flexibility in resourcing and the use of budgets.

Operational problems and issues

We here mean practical operating problems in any part of the organisation – and every department has them – or shortfalls in performance goals. It is likely that every problem in day-to-day life can be traced through to some inadequacy in capability – of employees, managers, leaders or teamworking. For HRD, every problem is an opportunity – to see how effective learning will transform performance.

Sources of problems may come from employee surveys, customer surveys, workplace behavioural problems, excessive attrition or absenteeism, safety or quality issues, business shortfalls, compliance failures, and so on. HRD should ensure they see the relevant reports and have a system for following them through.

Again, the same methodology described earlier can be applied. Its deployment prevents us from rushing to pet solutions, and helps us to focus on the right people and the right needs. Defining clearly the problem to be solved and the business measures we want to enhance sets the end objectives and the criteria for evaluation.

▌ EXAMPLE 2 (of the eight-step method)

This example is one of applying the methodology to an operational problem. The problem is defined as 'an unacceptable decrease in customer satisfaction'.

Step 1 is to define this more exactly in quantified terms, and Tables 3.4 and 3.5 show how this might develop.

Individual and team performance issues

The sister book in this series *Identifying of Training Needs* (Boydell *and* Leary 1996) discusses three levels of performance and need:

- *Level 1 Implementing* – doing things well

- *Level 2 Improving* – doing things better

- *Level 3 Innovating* – doing new and better things.

The first level is where there is a gap between the actual performance and the standard/desired/targeted performance. It is primarily about maintaining basic requirements, and may involve both standard 'initial' as well as remedial training.

The second is not just about individual improvement but the collective raising of standards. The third implies people who have sufficient mastery of the basics to begin

▷ Table 3.4 Example 2: Steps 1 and 2 – factors of influence

Business driver:	To restore an acceptable level of customer satisfaction.		
Quantified goal	Current state	Factors influencing the goal achievement	Relative importance of impact
Level of satisfaction with responsiveness to customer problems in Midlands area – target 8.5/10 in surveys; this level to be restored within 12 months	Currently 5.8; deteriorated from 6.9 six months ago and 8.2 twelve months ago	■ Call centre staffing ■ Engineer availability and turnover ■ Customer database reliability	25 60 15

Table 3.5 Example 2: Steps 3, 4 and 5 – people and their capability

Business driver	To restore an acceptable level of customer satisfaction.			
Key success factor	Engineer availability and turnover.			
Key people	Level of influence	Capability needed	Diag-nostic?	Is there a gap? How critical?
Customer service director	C	■ Achieving bottom-line targets with maintaining service levels ■ Motivating the CS team	no	This has got out of balance. He needs training and coaching, both in business planning and in motivating his team
Customer service planning manager	I	■ Ability to balance number of engineer sites with travel times promised to customers	no	Too cost driven – needs to understand customer perspective better and interaction between cost and service. Has cut engineering centres and caused much unrest
Engin-eering supervisors	C	■ Staff motivation ■ Customer relations ■ Planning and scheduling systems	yes	Due to restructuring, 50 per cent of supervisors are new and have no customer relationships. Older ones have difficulty coping with IT planning systems
Engineers	C	■ Using initiative to help customers ■ Influencing upwards	yes	Many engineers have left. Morale is low. Although most problems caused by others, engineers need resilience and sensitivity in dealing with irate customers

C= critical; I = important; H=helpful.

to question and massage them in order to create new avenues. These three levels are additive and require different learning modes.

This is a helpful classification when we come to look at performance needs – because we risk being locked into the first level without perhaps realising the potential of the others. Thus, even when things appear to be going well there is always a case of asking questions that relate to levels two and three. The classification also helps identify suitable learning objectives, modes and outcomes.

HRD will generally be keen to respond to requests for group performance needs, although we need care that we do not jump to the 'teambuilding' route to better performance. Most 'teambuilding' events are memorable experiences, either happy or traumatic ones, which leave their effect on the individuals concerned but *not* always on the performance of the organisation. This is because the goals are often unclear and unspecific, and in fact were about team motivation. This may well be a good investment, so long as we are clear as to what we are after.

Any solution to team performance that is built essentially around the people themselves is dependent on the network of their continuing relationships. Where a team learns to set directions, agree goals, define procedures, measure and monitor performance together, then these may endure independently of changes in the team members.

Generally, team training – where a group learns together – will be much more effective than occasional individual members being trained from time to time. Where serious bottom-line performance improvement is needed, this is the route to effective investment.

Managing *individual performance improvement* is a more difficult area, because no HRD department can attend to the needs of hundreds or thousands of individual employees. Here we rely on (a) processes of performance analysis (such as appraisals) and (b) our philosophy of responsibility for individual development. Most organisations continue to emphasise the key role of the manager as responsible for the development of their people, training them in coaching skills, and so on. Others recognise that if the real ownership could be placed with the individual themselves, then – given comprehensive support – a greater degree of success in improvement is likely. HRD's role is to provide the processes and much of the supporting skills and resources – as well as make the desired philosophy a cultural and everyday reality.

The world outside can change fast too

Our fourth reactive requirement is about demands placed on us from outside. In Chapter 2 we considered the general trends externally – but we may find we have to respond to some more immediate requirement.

SETTING USEFUL LEARNING GOALS AND OBJECTIVES

Learning goals are often set in a very vague way, and may be even just 'programme descriptions'. This is a critical activity. Learning goals have two parts:

1 the change in capability we are seeking

2 the impact this change will have on a business measure.

Sometimes the first part is sufficient. However, all that we derive using the eight-step method will be linked to a measurable impact, and this should make evaluation – if required – much easier.

Learning goals may be aimed at any of the components of capability described in the model in Figure 1.5. They may focus on extending a network of contacts or in providing a particular experience, as well as increasing knowledge and skills.

A knowledge and skills objective is a description of a performance the learners should be able to exhibit before they are considered 'competent'. An objective describes the intended results of learning instruction, rather than the process of learning itself. At the risk of stating the obvious, but it needs to be said, without clearly defined objectives it is impossible to determine whether they have actually been accomplished.

Programme objectives should clearly state what a learner ought to be able to *do* as a result of the learning experience. It has three components:

1 *Performance*. An objective describes what a learner is expected to be able to do.

2 *Conditions*. An objective describes the important conditions (if any) under which the performance is to occur.

3 *Criterion*. Whenever possible, an objective describes the criterion of acceptable performance by describing how well the learner must perform.

We return to this subject in Chapter 7, where we provide some examples of good programme objectives.

IN BRIEF

■ We distinguished three kinds of business goals for which HRD can take proactive action to see how learning can support them – current goals and strategies, organisation and human resource plans, and change initiatives. Since there is potentially a very wide range here, HRD needs to use judgement as to where the most needy cases may lie and focus on them.

- HRD needs a systematic method for linking strategic and business goals with the learning process. In this chapter we described an eight-step method that can be applied to any of the drivers. The secret of business-linked training and development is to be able to ask the right questions and be systematic in such methodologies.

- The group of *reactive* drivers includes performance and operational problems, in units and with teams or individuals, plus any external demands placed upon us. Whereas the business goals might not need HRD's help, it is almost certain that problems and issues of performance will need it in some way.

- We looked at the importance of setting clear learning goals, linking learning back to the business impact it is derived from. Not only will this help us to good and relevant learning solutions and avoid extraneous material, but it will also enable evaluation to take place without pain.

REFERENCES AND FURTHER READING

BOYDELL T. *and* LEARY M. (1996) *Identifying Training Needs*. London, IPD.

HEIDEMAN J. (1997) 'Writing performance objectives: Simple as A-B-C (and D).' In *The 1997 ASTD Training and Performance Yearbook*. Alexandria, Va, American Society of Training and Development.

MAGER R.F. (1984) *Preparing Instructional Objectives*. FT/Prentice Hall.

MAGER R.F. *and* PIPE P. (1991) *Analysing Performance Problems*. London, Kogan Page.

4 ■ STRATEGIES FOR PROFESSIONAL HRD MANAGEMENT

So far we have focused on the portfolio of *what* we should do in learning and development – and how our principles will be articulated in the form of policies. Now we have to make a set of choices about *how* we shall manage HRD; our own philosophies and approaches; and our processes and tools. We are on our own now – it's up to us to get these right as professionals – right in the sense of delivering most effectively within the culture and priorities of our unique organisation.

The focus of this chapter is on learning generally. However, our concern is about strategic choices; readers are referred to other books in the CIPD Training Essentials series for more in-depth 'how-to' advice. Chapter 5 looks at career and continuity management specifically, and the last three chapters examine resourcing, measuring and marketing.

In this chapter we shall cover:

■ strategic analysis, mission and vision

■ HRD's own beliefs and choices

■ people development processes and tools and learning methodologies.

STRATEGIC ANALYSIS, MISSION AND VISION

This sounds a bit grand for a support department. But it is always useful from time to time to analyse where we are and where we would like to be – even as individual people. The simplest tool for this is the familiar Strengths, Weaknesses, Opportunities and Threats analysis, simply expressed in four quadrants. Figure 4.1 gives an example. A full study would use subheadings, such as 'positioning and credibility', 'finance', 'skills and resources', 'business involvement', and so on. This analysis will in itself give

Figure 4.1   A SWOT analysis for an HR function

Strengths	Weaknesses
• expertise in management development • relationships with business schools • steering committee • programmes with high credibility • able to show good RoI • high external credibility	• lack of expertise in facilitation • generally weak business knowledge in staff • weak relationship with XX sector • lack of funds to meet all priorities • PDPs are shallow and bland
Opportunities	**Threats**
• new CFO is champion of knowledge management • CEO wants to create a true learning organisation • new intranet facilities • new OD strategy	• business downturn may mean budget cut • new CFO also keen on outsourcing as much as possible • loss of central training facility • new HRIS system unlikely to meet our needs

us a number of choices of action to take – within the context of what we want to be as a function (our mission) and where we want to get to (our vision). Should the HRD department have these of its own? It may be helpful, for the same reasons as an organisation finds it helpful – that is, if it is a meaningful 'anchor' to guide us. Some examples of mission statements from various organisations are as follows:

❝ We only exist to help our business units to produce better business results. We achieve this, in partnership with our clients, by developing the crucial aspects of individual, team and organisational business capability to improve the performance of all our people at work. ❞

❝ To create a comprehensive and integrated process for continuous learning which enables the Company to achieve the goals of its Mission Statement, and enables employees to a) develop their potential and b) make a direct contribution to the Company ❞

❝ To develop the skills and encourage the release of the potential of all employees in order to deliver customer driven continuous improvement. ❞

Here are some examples of Vision Statements:

'HRD is a business partner at every level of the organisation.'

'HRD adds at least three times more value than its cost.'

'Our company will become a true Learning Organisation; our people will be the best in the industry world-wide and will be delighted by their personal growth and development during their career with the Company.'

As we said in Chapter 2, these statements need an appropriate measure to see whether we are making progress towards the vision. We may also have some long-term *goals* relating to aspects of HRD as a function, and aspects of our achievements for human capital growth:

- return on investment (RoI) of HRD spend
- share of overall company training spend
- resource profile and utilisation
- client feedback parameters

and for people development in the organisation:

- core competency levels of expertise
- leadership capability
- succession capability.

HRD'S OWN BELIEFS AND CHOICES

HRD's own beliefs and methodologies will be strongly shaped by the values and philosophy of the organisation itself, although sometimes it strikes out on its own path for better or worse. It may fill a void by designing and publishing documents expressing its best understanding of the strategy the organisation wishes to pursue. The personal beliefs, experience and passions of the HRD director and/or his or her boss are bound to influence this. Although we are being somewhat clinical in our systematic approach in this book, it is worth remembering how many passionate, even evangelistic, HRD directors have had a radical influence on their organisation.

▷ Table 4.1 HRD behaviours supporting typical organisational values

Value	Positive behaviours	Negative behaviours
Excellence	■ Professional quality of administration ■ Highly positive event feedback ■ Quality of materials	■ Trainers not keeping to their objectives ■ Lack of information ■ Sloppy poorly prepared support materials
Customer focus	■ Trainees as customers – meeting their needs is the priority ■ All events focus on/ refer to external customers ■ Delegate feedback is taken seriously and responded to	■ The department's focus is on its own efficiency and convenience ■ External customers do not feature in most events ■ Obtaining feedback is no more than a routine exercise
Self-development	■ Systems for training and development start from the principle of personal ownership by individual employees ■ Programmes always feature personal actions before, during and after an event ■ HRD staff set an example through their continuous personal development	■ Programmes are essentially trainer driven ■ Little or no resource is put into self-development centres or helping people evaluate their development needs ■ Systems and processes feature the manager as the prime decision maker in people development
Achievement	■ The HRD function has a clear set of measures, continually monitored ■ Individual department members are stretched to perform ■ Systems are in place to measure learning achievement	■ Poor performance is tolerated and not dealt with in the department ■ Activities themselves are more important than what they achieve ■ No interest is taken in the organisation's business goals and achievements

Values for HRD departments

One key role of HRD is to support and bring alive the organisation's values.

Rather than create additional new values of its own, HRD should define behaviours that exemplify their own living of the existing values. Table 4.1 gives some examples.

▋ APPLICATION

What values do you have in your organisation and how does (could) HRD exemplify them in their activities?

Here are some of the choices HRD has to make:

Training vs learning

Although 'learning' is the word on everyone's lips, in practice most HRD functions still have a heavy emphasis on the design and delivery of events – maybe using a variety of learning techniques within them. Training is a vital part of the overall learning process, and it is not a question of one or the other. However, it is recognised that 80+ per cent of our learning comes from experience and work itself, and at most 20 per cent from off-the-job events – however, the effort and attention devoted by HRD functions is generally the inverse of this. Whereas training is event, 'teacher', and solution centred, learning is process, 'learner' and problem oriented. A true concern for learning will take us much more out of the classroom and out of 'content design', and into the workplace. It will significantly influence the skills we need in the team – more coaching of others in learning processes and less upfront delivery skills.

▋ APPLICATION

Analyse the total time that the HRD function spends against different learning activities. How much is directly linked to off-the-job events? Does this reflect a true commitment to learning?

We should expect HRD professionals to be experts in the learning process and to be coaches of others in it.

The role of the manager – control or support?

HRD people continue to stress the manager's role in developing their people. In many organisations a tremendous effort has gone into insisting managers have training in coaching skills in order to encourage this role. One sometimes thinks that if managers all came up to the specification of HR's ideal people manager, they certainly wouldn't have time for any business activities.

Although there are always role models, the reality is that, in many cultures, a minority of managers actually exhibit, or have the time, to show good coaching and development skills. This traditional hierarchical model of what a manager should do is flawed. Of course a manager always has a role to play, but it is not necessarily controlling and directing the development of other people. It should be supporting the needs and plans of his or her people, ensuring they get feedback (not necessarily giving it exclusively), and using work opportunities to grow people.

If the individuals who have the learning needs can be helped to manage their own learning processes and be skilled at calling on support from their manager or team leader as necessary, then we have a different dynamic.

The 'ideal' manager-developer is characterised by:

- ensuring that business goals have supporting learning goals as needed
- ensuring all staff assigned to him/her are trained in managing their own learning
- ensuring each person has a personal development plan that is realistic and agreed
- providing time and money for agreed development plans to be implemented
- ensuring pre- and post-discussions re learning events for team members take place
- providing and receiving constructive feedback
- ensuring systems of working, include systematic learning from daily work
- ensuring knowledge and experience is shared within the group and with other appropriate groups
- sharing what is happening in their own job
- being a role model – of the company values, and of good management
- being available as a coach and guide where this is needed
- using work opportunities to develop others; delegating wherever possible
- showing concern for how the team functions as a team
- permitting risk-taking and focusing on learning if things go wrong
- safeguarding budgetary allocations put aside for learning.

The question for HRD is how to ensure managers and staff have all the knowledge,

Figure 4.2 Stakeholders in the organisation's people development

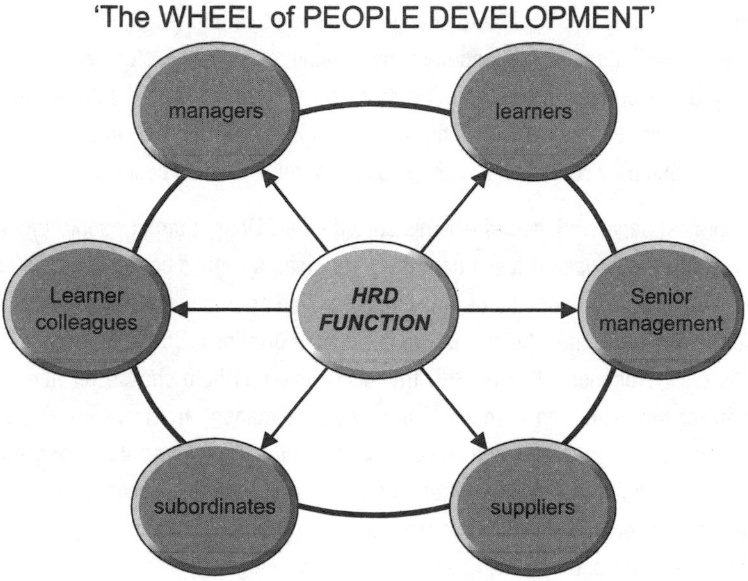

'The WHEEL of PEOPLE DEVELOPMENT'

managers

learners

Learner colleagues

HRD FUNCTION

Senior management

subordinates

suppliers

information and skills needed to support this self-sufficient model, and particularly in the disciplines of rigorous systematic learning from work experiences.

Glorious isolation or systems thinking? Roles and skills in the overall people development process

The HRD function cannot sit in isolation (perhaps in its own country house); it is but the hub of the wheel of people development. There are several stakeholder groups in the process – see Figure 4.2 – and each plays a different role. We should define that role and make sure the people involved understand and accept them. We discussed the role of managers in the previous section, but should do the same for each group. Along with the roles are specific knowledge, skills and behaviours that enable the role to be fulfilled.

APPLICATION

Draw up a map of the stakeholders in HRD in your organisation. Summarise their key roles in the learning process and the skills they need to carry them out.

Training schedules vs customised learning solutions

Often there is an *expectation* from much of the organisation for a catalogue of training events, and it takes a long time to change this to custom-built solutions. In one of my roles as an HRD director, I abandoned the catalogue, as a result of my 'progressive thinking' about problem-based learning. It was a failure – people did not understand what we meant. It made me realise how difficult it is to create a real culture of 'thinking learning' – and how conditioned managers are to 'think training courses'.

The appraisal paperwork can affect this considerably. Does it direct people towards a course solution? Or does it focus on getting the need specified correctly and choosing from a range of solutions? If the answer is derived from current or previous course catalogues it perpetuates the status quo in terms of offerings. On the other hand, if the need is clearly defined, HRD or HRD-trained people can help choose an appropriate solution for the need. The former is much easier to manage from everyone's point of view. Unfortunately it results in a lot of wasted training days where the wrong solution meets an ill-defined need. It often leads to the cheerful acceptance of quite inappropriate event members. This is bad news for everybody – wasted days of training, frustration for tutors, for participants, and for other delegates.

The question for HRD is: 'What are our criteria of success?' The pressures to fill advertised events may be significant – resource productivity, committed costs or target numbers. Are we driven by numbers or by measured learning achievement? It may be argued that it is impossible to check every event thoroughly for the latter. Once again, however, the answer lies in the *process* – in the questions asked and in the competence of individuals themselves in managing their learning.

We shall always have course solutions, some of which we shall run for a long time as part of our umbrella strategy. But what percentage of our activities is pre-scheduled, and does it reflect the real priorities?

PEOPLE DEVELOPMENT PROCESSES AND TOOLS

Whenever we create or review our HRD strategy we need to ask whether we have the best processes for supporting people development, and also look at the tools we are, or could be, using. Some caution is needed on the latter, lest we be led into temptation. The market is brimming over with tools to be used in assessment of personality, of motivation, of career interest, of potential, of culture; and questionnaires of all kinds for feedback, self-awareness and personal effectiveness. Many are of great value – but we need to be discriminating and find a few that work for our culture and stay with them.

The most important process of all is the 'eight-step' method, or equivalent – the link between the business and learning. Career development and succession are examined in the next chapter; here we are going to discuss the processes of:

- performance and development reviews
- personal development planning
- job induction
- knowledge management

and the following tools:

- capability frameworks
- role and personal profiles
- multi-input feedback
- diagnostics
- development and assessment centres.

The fundamental processes of performance and development review

The most significant source of individual development needs is performance appraisal. It is amazing how a process that has been around for some 40 years is continuously a source of concern to organisations, constantly being re-engineered. The objectives of many systems are confused, and the development outcome may take second place to the determination of a pay decision. Two distinctly different processes are involved – one to assess *performance* against some expectations or targets; the other to look at *capability,* the strengths and weaknesses that lie behind the performance.

Some organisations separate the two physically and request two reviews. Others combine them. The HRD director would want to be sure that the *development* discussion is not being compromised or diluted in any way. He or she will also be concerned about the *range* of feedback involved in the process. The traditional manager–employee appraisal is fine for discussing achievements, but severely limited in its ability to cover the whole range of performance, especially the area of personal skills. The job itself is the richest source of learning – therefore analysing and understanding work performance is very important, arguably far more so than the artificiality of development centres.

HRD is usually going to be involved, if not lead, in the design of appraisal and related processes. It is a fundamental platform in people development that has a significant contribution to the dialogue between individuals and the organisation they work for. There are many aspects of their design that will give clear messages about the values of the organisation, and therefore deserve much thought. Many excellent books are available to help, but here are some of the key design questions:

- What are the desired outcomes and who 'owns' them?

- Who will be involved in the process, and how?

- Do we want to use it to reinforce the organisation's values?

- Shall we rate performance, and if so, how?

- How will it link to our capability framework?

- Will there be interim reviews?

- Will there be discussion/anything written about potential?

Most organisations would see this process as a cornerstone of *performance management* – of cascading strategic objectives down to individuals, and of enabling performance improvement. That improvement comes through advice and counsel from the appraiser, and from agreed development actions. However, apart from extreme examples of poor performance under the spotlight, many organisations would be hard pressed to show that their appraisal system improves performance overall. It cannot be shown by average increases in 'ratings' – there is a natural drift in these and few indeed stand up to objective analysis of consistency. Some organisations have 90+ per cent (especially in the public sector) of their people as very good or excellent. It is also difficult to show improvement because managers are imprecise in setting development objectives, and in linking them to a performance outcome.

APPLICATION

What are the desired outcomes of your appraisal/development processes?
Are the development outcomes compromised or sub-optimised in any way?
How could you ensure that they contribute more effectively to the real development of the individual and his/her performance?

'Personal development plans' – the difference between training and learning plans

For a comprehensive study of training needs analysis, readers are referred to the companion volume in this 'Training Essentials' series with that title. When it comes to individuals, the question is whether plans are driven by the solution provider or by the learner. In a traditional appraisal model, at the end of the discussion the manager studied a list of training courses available and chose some for the appraisee to attend in the coming year. This choice was loosely based on the manager's personal perception of need; plus the appraisee's desire for what interested him or her, *plus what was available*. The training manager received copies of the appropriate page of the appraisal in order to formulate the demand for the catalogue they had already produced. The result was:

- learning solutions were conditioned by the types of course available

- managers were often unskilled in the definition of learning objectives and chose courses for a variety of reasons ('you haven't been on this one yet'; 'this will make a nice change for you', 'this looks about right for the problem we discussed', etc)

- employees waited to be given the opportunity to attend

- training was a programming activity, and self-perpetuating.

This still happens, and one is amazed at the number of new appraisal systems that still talk exclusively about 'training' in the development section.

There is certainly a place for a catalogue of courses, particularly those concerned with know-how. But this approach produces an immense amount of wasted training days (at least from the business point of view), and – worse – often fails to meet vital learning needs.

The personal development plan (PDP) has many advantages in comparison. This is not an integral part of an appraisal form to be filed away, but a live and current document owned by individuals themselves. A good design will focus attention on setting clear learning objectives, on choosing from a range of learning methodologies, and be prioritised according to practical realities. It should be designed to be *owned* by the individual, with management in a supporting role.

A typical personal development plan might have four separate inputs, of needs arising from:

- *performance*. This will be through the appraisal process or other work-based discussions.

- *new requirements* in the current role. This requires a dialogue with management as to how the role will develop, need new knowledge or skills, or even prepare for the situation where it may disappear altogether.

- *career aspirations.* These would be seeking opportunities for capability enhancements without necessarily changing the current role, which would help growth towards a target future job.

- desires for *personal development* unconnected with the other categories. The willingness to allow these will depend on the breadth of the organisation's overall beliefs in people development.

Personal development plans should clearly state who is responsible for each action and when it will happen. Of course, they have to be reviewed because development is ongoing – preferably two or three times a year.

The way such plans are implemented will reflect the approach to personal ownership and self-management of learning. Implementation may be left in the hands of the manager to initiate as appropriate, or with the individual. If the latter, some negotiation of time and money is needed before ownership can be real, as well as some training in the skills needed for self-management.

A note on self-managed learning

The arguments for self-managed learning are very strong. A strategic decision to encourage this has several implications, and considerable thought by HRD is needed. It is mere abdication to tell employees bluntly, 'in this company you are responsible for your own development; here is some money and here is a booklet to guide you'. People need to understand why it is in their interest, be motivated to spend time on themselves, and be trained in managing the processes of learning.

Every employee needs to be able to:

- articulate good learning objectives (see page 81)

- understand their learning style (see below)

- understand how the learning cycle works (see below)

- be aware of the range of learning modes available and how to make the right choice for their need

- be a good 'coachee'

- be able to give and receive feedback constructively

- be a sharer of knowledge and a user of other people's knowledge.

Managers also need skills to provide the necessary level of support, as described in the above section on the manager's role.

If self-management is chosen, then the organisation may consider some computerised tools to help employees. For example, in organisations like Hewlett Packard and Sun Microsystems people can determine their own profiles and match them electronically against any job in the company. Furthermore, when a capability gap is identified that should be met by a training course, they can access the courses available and book themselves on what they want without leaving their screen.

The process can be helped forward by setting up and facilitating 'self-managed learning groups'. Here, individuals interested in their own learning share their needs and progress and use each other for help. The practical difficulties of self-managed learning can be shared and explored. Readers are referred to Megginson and Whittaker's *Cultivating Self Development* for guidance on how this can be done effectively.

How do we do 'Induction'?

The normal accounting system has many inadequacies, one of which is its inability to tell us about 'hidden costs'. One of these is the inefficiency of 'learning curves' that happen when people change jobs.

Induction is often seen only as a welcoming and communicating ritual managed by HR, or left to department managers for *new* employees. New graduates may get something much more thorough, but what is often missing is systematic *job* induction. This is needed for every job change, not just new employees. This has to be a concern for HRD.

What is needed is a systematic framework for designing job induction programmes, and people trained to do them. It may take half a day to write such a programme, but accelerate the learning curve by 50 per cent compared with the haphazard 'get stuck in and learn as we go' approach.

One effective approach is to divide a programme into sections, and each would have:

- learning objectives
- reference material/people
- self-managed learning assignments, studying the materials and talking with key people
- review questions to check understanding.

Well constructed, this format helps the individual to understand quickly the issues surrounding the job; know where to look for things subsequently; and have already thought through some of the challenges ahead. The manager plays a major role in

▷ Table 4.2 Extracts from an induction programme

Management development consultant
Contents
1   Welcome; the context and importance of this post
2   Main accountabilities and parameters
3   Company knowledge
4   The human resources function
5   Management development in the company
6   Priorities and objectives for the future

Sample Section: 5, MANAGEMENT DEVELOPMENT IN THE COMPANY
Learning objective: To bring you up to date with the history and current state of management development policy and practice; to enable you to assess where we are and where we should be heading, and thereby to formulate objectives to aim for.
References:
People: Mr A, previous incumbent
            Ms B, Personnel Director
            Mr C, Chief Executive
            Mr D, Head of Training
            Ms E, External Consultant, ABC Ltd
            Mr F, International Sales Director
            Ms G, Training and Development Manager, main subsidiary
Material: R1 Management Development Policy
            R2 Performance Appraisal System
            R3 Succession Planning Database
            R4 Career Structures Manual
            R5 Standards for use of Assessment Centres
            R6 Career Counselling Course material
            R7 Organisation Review Committee minutes
Learning assignments:
1   Study R1, R3 and R7. To what extent are the objectives outlines in R1 being met in practice? What seems to be missing? Does R3 give any indication of problem areas – where are they?
2   Arrange to see Mr C and discuss with him his vision of the future and the characteristics of the managers that will be needed. Discuss also your findings from the previous assignment to see which are of concern to him.
3   Discuss with Mr A his view of his successes and failures; achievements and frustrations. Study R3 and ask him about any queries you have; how it was used, and how it needs developing. What would be Mr A's objectives in the next year if he was still in the job?
4   Discuss with Mr F the needs of the international part of the business as he sees them. How do they match up with current policy and practice? Make notes on issues of concern.
5   Meet with Ms G and similar colleagues, having first made a checklist of items to ask about regarding local practice. What are their expectations of your role? What local initiatives are being undertaken? How does their practice match up to R1? Ask them about R2 – how comfortable are managers with it? How useful are the outputs in people development actions? Are managers well trained in this area?

▷ Table 4.2 – continued

6   Meet Ms E and discuss the work that is being done with the organisation on development centres. Make notes on their history, their design and the challenges she sees regarding their future development. Go through R5 with her, and note any problem areas.

7   Discuss with Mr D how training for management is commissioned and designed, implemented and evaluated. What role should you play in this specification of off-the-job learning events? Which courses are the most popular and why? Which are shown to have the greatest value in improved job performance?

8   Study R6, and in discussions with Ms G and others assess how valuable it is. Are the messages consistent with the needs expresses by the people you have met?

9   Arrange to spend at least half a day with Ms B. Prepare beforehand an agenda for discussion. It should include the history of the various processes and committees in operation; the political aspects of succession; the inputs received from your various contacts, and your preliminary ideas for priorities in the job.

Questions to check understanding (some examples):

■   What innovations in management development in XXX Division were introduced in 1998?

■   Where do we have a real problem in medium-term succession?)

                    Adapted from Mayo, A.J. *Managing Careers*, IPM, 1992, pp298–301.

guiding the person through this period and reviewing progress from time to time – even though managing the assignments is self-directed. This needs to be a *full-time* occupation and not confused (wherever possible) with getting started in the job at the same time. Most jobs *can* wait another two or three weeks to get started.

Table 4.2 shows an extract from a real programme written for a management development consultant coming from outside the company.

APPLICATION

What systems are in use in your organisation for both external and internal induction? What is their coverage in time and content? To what extent are they self-managed?

In what ways do you feel that a more thorough approach would be beneficial to the organisation?

Knowledge management – is it HRD's problem?

Many HR and HRD functions have little to do with knowledge management (KM) initiatives. Indeed, when the UK's *Human Resources* magazine started their 'Excellence Awards' in 2000 they had a category for 'contribution to knowledge management', but after two years had to abandon it for lack of submissions.

Is knowledge anything to do with people? A silly question – but the answer leads us inevitably to the conclusion that 'managing knowledge effectively' must be the concern of HRD. It is closely allied to 'organisational learning', a fundamental part of a learning organisation. Often owned and driven by the IT department, research has consistently shown that success is 80 per cent due to people factors – such as:

- the willingness to share knowledge

- the willingness to utilise the knowledge and experience of others

- the supporting culture – its openness, whether it is blame-free, its acceptance of mistakes

- providing the time necessary, and so on.

What should HRD's strategy be here? It starts from at least supporting and being an integral part of any initiatives that are ongoing, and may even stretch to catalysing the initiative itself. This is a big subject for a small book, but some questions for HRD to ask are the following:

- What skills are needed to manage and exchange knowledge effectively, and how should these be provided?

- What is our role in promoting/facilitating 'communities of practice'?

- Do we have a role in 'key knowledge asset mapping'?

- When we make acquisitions and alliances, is it our job to understand and protect the new knowledge assets?

- How much time is put into our events for people to learn from each other, sharing successes and mistakes?

- How can we utilise KM tools, such as the intranet and virtual discussion, to spread and encourage learning?

- What kind of tool should we have to find who in the organisation might have a particular capability?

- Do we build in the *transfer* of learning to others as an outcome from events?

- How do we ensure that learning from the external world is brought into the right places internally?

- Do we need a cultural change programme to change processes and behaviours that get in the way of open knowledge sharing?

In Chapter 7 we outline a way to make the business case for knowledge management.

CLASSIC HRD TOOLS

The importance of capability frameworks

Many 'competency frameworks' are limited in scope and limited in application. They are frequently confined to behavioural skills only, as if this is all that capability is about, with perhaps a catch-all 'technical and professional skills'. HR has learnt an enormous amount about behavioural skills and their assessment over the past 10 years, but has in many cases lost touch with the reality of what jobs are about. Watch a line manager interview and see what he or she wants to know about. Most of the time will be spent exploring technical knowledge, experiences, successes, failures, contacts and so on. They will also look behind these experiences for how they were achieved, but still rely a lot – in the end – on their feeling of 'fit'.

A complete capability dictionary, with discrimination between levels, is an essential tool for all the processes of matching people and jobs – whether the job they are in, or a job they are being considered for. This common language forms the basis of profiling and assessment. Figure 4.3 illustrates the uses of such a framework.

HRD is involved in many of these processes. It should own this vital tool, which should pass the following tests:

Figure 4.3 Capability as the core of people matching processes

- It should be *practical* to use by all employees and managers – not require specialist help to understand its complexity.

- It should be *useful* in making key processes work – a means to an end and not an end in itself.

- It should be *flexible* and adaptable, applicable to many different environments or situations – not a universal formula.

- It should enable *distinctions* between levels of requirement to be made – but simply, and not requiring complex assessment procedures.

There are many models of competency available, varying particularly in their approaches to distinctions between levels.

In Chapter 1, we outlined a comprehensive model of capability in Figure 1.5. It shows two foundational components on which others are built – qualifications and experience. Then we have business, technical and professional know-how, which embraces knowledge and specialised skills; personal skills – which is the substance of most 'competency frameworks'; and 'know-who', the network of contacts that are critical to success in many jobs. These are embraced by the values and attitudes the individual holds.

Educational levels and professional qualifications

There has been an explosive growth in 'certification', driven by governments rather than employers. Indeed, the latter are often sceptical about the benefit to them of many qualifications. Since many institutions are reluctant to fail students, the grades achieved are more important than the certificate itself.

A professional (or regulatory) qualification may be necessary to give a licence to practice. In measurement terms it is simple – the certificate, or a certain grade, was or was not achieved. For some organisations as a whole, or for some parts of organisations, this may have special importance. In an R&D environment, the percentage of people with higher degrees may be a critical measure and a benchmark against competition, or in finance, where the percentage who are fully qualified is a measure of departmental strength.

Experiences

Experiences are the real foundation of learning. Experience gives us both breadth and depth of other competencies, and has value in its own right. It is relatively easy to measure – it has happened or not happened factually. Experiences may or may not be successful in achievement terms, but still can enhance other capabilities. They are obtained through the following:

▷ Table 4.3 Levels of experience

Experience area	Level	Time spent	Scope/stretch	Size
Project management (*Delivering discrete results using resources 'owned' by others*)	1	<1 year	Internal, own department	Budget <£10K; length <3 months
	2	1–2 years	External, own department	£10–100K; 3–6 months
	3	2–5 years	Internal, cross-department	£100–500K; 6–12 months
	4	>5 years	External, multifunctional	>£500K; >12 months
International role (*working in contact with, or located in other countries*)	1	<1 year	Regular liaison with people from other countries	1–5 countries; involvement; or technical/profession al secondment
	2	1–2 years	Responsibility for resources abroad; frequent visits	6–12 countries; or management secondment (developed world)
	3	2–5 years	One international secondment	13–30 countries; or management secondment (less developed world)
	4	>5 years	Several international secondments	globally or country leadership

■ being accountable in a function for some results or value added

■ being in a particular type of situation and coping with it

■ a particular type of project, and learning from it

■ a particular type of problem or opportunity that has been confronted.

We need some parameters to describe experiences. Three key indicators are:

■ time spent – how long has been spent in a situation or job type

■ scope and stretch – how complex was the experience

■ parameters of size – revenues, people, countries, etc.

For example, if we want to distinguish levels of experience in project management, or in international roles, we might draw up a guide as in Table 4.3. A development or

▲ Table 4.4 The experience profile of a team

Area of experience	Entry			When experienced			Person A			Person B			Person C		
	time	sc	sz	time	sc	sz	time	sc	sz	time	sc	sz	time	sc	sz
International management	—	—	—	2+	2	1	3	3	2	2	2	2	4	3	3
Product marketing	2	1	1	3+	3+	3	2	3	3	2	1	1	4	4	3
Distribution channels	1	1	1	3+	3+	3	3	2	2	1	2	1	3	3	3
Pricing	1	1	1	3+	3+	3	2	3	3	1	2	1	4	3	3

sc = scope; sz = size.

recruitment programme aimed at growing the experience of a team may then track its success using a format as in Table 4.4.

Technical, professional and business know-how

A large amount of training has this area as its objective. It includes both *knowledge* and *professional skills.* The latter overlaps with 'personal skills' but covers those where specific training is needed to be competent (as opposed to many personal behaviours).

We need to distinguish *levels* of expertise. A helpful and simple approach is to make a judgement on this five-point scale for a defined field of knowledge or skill:

A = 'Aware' – can speak the language; knows what is involved

B = 'Basic' – has a rudimentary knowledge of the field

C = 'Competent' – is able to discuss and work competently

D = 'Distinguished' – is one to whom work colleagues turn for advice

E = 'Expert' – is known within and beyond the organisation for his/her expertise

This scale embraces 'practical expertise' just as much as intellectual knowledge.

Philips, the international electronics company, uses a variation of this scale. Their four levels are:

1   Foundation

2   Practitioner

3   Expert

4   Leader.

For a particular area of expertise, these levels can be expanded to describe what is required at each level.

Many programmes will have their goals described as achieving a certain level, eg 'To provide participants with the areas of knowledge defined at Level C.' The achievement can be tested in several ways – by actual examinations, by oral tests, or in practice.

Longer-term programmes may have objectives such as 'achieving a certain number of, or percentage of, people with "D" or "E" levels'.

Personal skills

This covers personal traits, attitudes and behaviours that are demanded by a role, or which generally characterise 'high performance'. They are undoubtedly important and very individual. They are difficult to assess in an objective and consistent way.

The behaviours that go with the organisation's values would be a core set applicable to every employee. They are 'the passport to working here'.

Personal behaviours are described in different ways. Here are some examples taken from various companies' competency frameworks:

■ a description of behaviours represented by the competency

■ a description of positive and negative examples of the behaviour

■ hierarchical levels of expectation of the behaviour – typically three to four levels from that expected of all employees to that which is expected of leaders

■ levels of demonstration of the behaviour – but not linked hierarchically.

People do not behave consistently in different situations or at different times, and more mature demonstrations are to be expected in senior roles. However, quite junior people can display high levels of some behaviours, if given the chance.

A useful approach to describing behaviours is to specify a series of specific examples of them at each level and against which individuals can be assessed for both strength and consistency.

Assessment can be done in three ways:

■ on-the-job observation, assessed in performance appraisals

■ on-the-job observation using feedback instruments such as '360°' surveys

■ off-the-job observation, through targeted assessment centres.

Psychological tests indicate the *likelihood* of behaviours being shown, but people adapt to situations, so these are not as reliable a guide as real observation. They can be useful in recruitment when people are not known internally.

Personal network – 'know–who'

'Who you know' can be as important – if not more so (in some jobs) – than 'what you know'. Many development programmes will have an objective of extending internal or external networks.

Depending on the nature of the organisation's activities, we might have some useful measures such as:

■ proportion of customers known personally

■ number of prospects we have based on a personal relationship

■ number of competitors with whom we have a personal link

- number of relevant officials known

- number of relevant experts outside the organisation who are known

- range of contacts in other divisions, departments, countries

- number of employees with management potential who are known (a measure for a management development manager).

This aspect of capability can be described in the following ways:

- extent of network:

  - level of contacts (upwards, downwards, sideways)

  - internal/external balance

  - national/international

- variety of contacts, eg business, political, government, professional, academic

- quality and relevance of relationships:

  - business acquaintance, business provider, social acquaintance, etc

  - strength – how likely they are to help

  - degree of influence.

An index can be created based on a combination of relevant items and using a five-point scale to provide discrimination of the extent of this capability.

APPLICATION

If you have a capability (or competency) framework, how and where is it used? How might you extend its application and influences to new processes and new groups of employees?

Role and personal profiles

The design of these is important to HRD since they will form the practical basis of the matching processes. Some suggestions are:

- All role descriptions should distinguish between the *essential* entry criteria and the *maturity levels* that the role potentially brings. The latter are the levels that could generally be expected through doing the job for its normal lifespan. Some may exceed these, but the point is that the difference between the two levels gives us a *learning opportunity,* which particularly helps in career planning.

■ As roles become more senior, and people become more experienced, experience and network play a greater significance, both in the needs of a role and in the value that a person may contribute.

■ Individuals should keep a personal capability profile constantly up to date, which summarises their distinctive and *cumulative* capabilities in each of the components. It is important to include those gained previously, since people tend to be pigeonholed based on the job they are seen to do.

■ Everyone should be able to show some positive change in their personal profile year on year, and it should be reviewed at the development discussion.

Multi-input feedback

Feedback is an essential form of learning. The people who see the true '*how*' of performance are other team members, subordinates, colleagues and customers (internal or external) – and much of what they see is hidden from the nominal boss. For development purposes, some form of 'multi-input' or 360° appraisal process has great benefit – and not just for managers. Normally anonymity is guaranteed, but HR departments can be over-sensitive about the potential dangers of open one-to-one feedback. There is a good argument that people should be able to make their own choice of *how* feedback should be provided, and their own choice as to whether it should be open. My own personal experience of complete openness was immensely valuable and I do not believe it affected the honesty of respondees.

The HRD director has to decide:

■ In what contexts do we want to use multi-input feedback and what would be our objectives? They could be used for self-awareness, for development planning, for competency appraisal, for knowledge about peer perception, for assessing potential, for checking aggregate leadership capability – and no doubt others.

■ For whom shall we recommend it? This depends on the answers above – but it can be used for every employee.

■ Will it be mandatory or voluntary? Provided any suspicions are removed, most people welcome this kind of feedback. In its early use it may be made voluntary.

■ How shall we communicate its use? This is critically important.

■ What tools shall we use? Beware immensely complicated multi-factor tools. The tools should preferably be customised to embrace the values and key competences of *your* organisation.

■ How shall we manage feedback? There are many options of choice. There are advantages in the external person who can be dispassionate, but who may be less helpful due to lack of knowledge of the organisation.

■ What happens to the data? One argument is that only one copy should be made, and kept by the employee. But it depends on the purpose of the exercise.

■ Shall we use it regularly or once only? This depends on the answer to the first point.

Diagnostic instruments

A great variety of diagnostic instruments are on the market, available for use by individuals, teams and organisational units. The HRD director will be wise to control their use so that useful data can be compiled, for comparisons between units and over time. A particularly useful set is published by Peter Honey, including Honey and Mumford's well-known questionnaire on learning styles, developed in the mid-1980s and a bestseller ever since (see his website, listed in References and Further Reading). Based on Kolb's learning cycle, it identifies four styles.

■ *Activist.* Open minded, enthusiastic, enjoys the challenge of new experiences, tends to act first and consider consequences afterwards. Happiest with activity.

■ *Reflector.* Enjoys analysis, collecting data, pondering the implications of experiences. Good listener and observer of others. Not the fastest decision taker.

■ *Theorist.* Adapts and integrates observations into models and theories; thinks problems through logically; enjoys synthesis as well as analysis. Rationality and logic matter most.

■ *Pragmatist.* Looks for new ideas, likes experimentation to see what works in practice. Impatient with long discussions, practical down-to-earth problem solver.

Amongst their wide range of instruments is also one assessing how good a manager is at managing a learning environment, useful in developing towards a learning organisation.

There are many cultural assessment questionnaires available, but – as for 360° feedback – there is much to be said for customising them to your own organisation.

Development and assessment centres

Originally designed for the purposes of selection, these have become a widely used tool, for various assessment purposes and for self-insight and development. It is an expensive and over-used process, which often lacks today the inherent integrity of design and evaluation that is essential. The risks are that too many competencies are attempted for assessment with inadequate coverage of each, observed by untrained assessors, and evaluated mechanically in the final session. This process has immense potential value but should be used only where what is already known is considered to be inadequate. Graduate selection is a clear case; supplementing the appraisal to find development needs is often not.

The HRD director will need to decide, depending on the purpose of any particular centre:

- Where, when and for what purposes will these tools be used?

- What standards of integrity will be laid down?

- Shall we use internal or external assessors?

- How will training be given to internal assessors and facilitators?

- How will exercises and simulations be managed to avoid overuse?

- How will the results be integrated with other relevant information?

- How will the data be kept and used?

DESIGN OF LEARNING PROCESSES

Going round the learning cycle

The different modes of learning are covered well in companion 'Training Essentials' books and in Alan Mumford's excellent *How to Choose a Development Method* (1997). These need to be supplemented by a good understanding of e-learning options – see References and Further Reading.

If there is one tool that should be at the heart of the HRD director's thinking it is probably the 'learning cycle' (see Figure 4.4), the need to take people around it until the desired learning is embedded in changed behaviour. For many learning needs, this will lead us to a *series* of components of a learning process, only one or two of which might be classroom based.

What we might call 'end-to-end' solutions should be our goal. This means that:

- we are confident that the learning need was identified systematically

- it has been translated into specific learning objectives

- we are able to design the learning process that will most effectively achieve these objectives

- we are able to ensure that the application of the learning takes place and to be satisfied that the need is a need no longer

- we have planned for the transfer of relevant learning to others

Figure 4.4 The cycle of effective learning

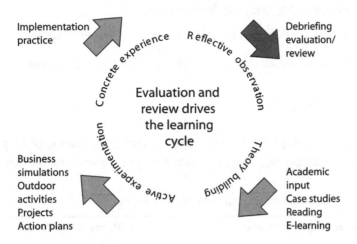

This takes us beyond formal programmes, and into the concept of internal 'learning partnerships'. It involves working with managers and learners, both before and after a formal event. In practice, this cannot be done with every course delegate, so a systematic process that enables the necessary steps to take place is needed. Hence the importance of the generic learning events for all employees on 'effective learning management'.

Learning solutions and their application

We outlined in Chapter 1 four modes of learning, as follows:

- *education* – changing the way people think, providing new knowledge

- *training* – enabling people to do things differently, or to do new things

- *learning from others* – being coached or mentored, tapping into knowledge databases and the tacit knowledge of people we interface with

- *learning from experiences* – generally work based.

A total learning process might include all these elements. For example, a programme of change management might include:

- learning from books or in the classroom about a change model and the routes to success and failure

- practical role playing and feedback of helping people through 'transitions'

- systematically talking to two or three people who have recently been through major change, and learning their lessons

- planning and implementing a job-based change using the agreed model

- reviewing what happened with fellow learners

- revising the model that the learner knows works for them personally.

This might have an elapsed time of six months or more, for all the components.

Sources of learning

Application of learning back in the workplace is often left to chance, or the parting exhortation to 'discuss what you have learnt with your manager'. Part of knowledge

▷ Table 4.5 Sources of learning and means of application

Type of learning	Sources	Means of transfer or application
New knowledge	Reading/e-learning program Courses and programmes Seminars and conferences Personal discussion	Seminars, meetings Reports, summaries, papers Groupware, intranet Application to decisions, and actions
New/enhanced skills	Coaching, imitation Training courses and programmes Experimentation	Skills used in practice
Changed attitudes	Training courses and workshops Reading and personal study Influence of individuals Experience	Influencing others Application to actions and decisions Changed behaviour
New experience	Situations Projects Problem-solving Action learning	Presentations Reports, summaries, papers Groupware, intranet 'Communities of practice'
Increased network	Courses and programmes Seminars and conferences Use of Internet Professional associates	Drawing on experience and best practice Ongoing sharing through meetings/Internet

management is the transfer of knowledge and learning to others, and this is rarely evaluated. It should be an integral part of the overall learning design. Table 4.5 provides some thoughts regarding options for learning and its subsequent transfer.

APPLICATION

Draw up a table like that in Table 4.5 for a selection of current HRD activities with which you are involved.

IN BRIEF

- HRD should do its own SWOT analyses, to assess its position and its potential strategies as a function. It may or may not choose to have its own mission and vision, but its values should be those of the organisation and consciously role modelled.

- HRD should not only be experts in learning, but also be able to coach and advise others. They will be particularly concerned with the roles and skills of others in the learning process, and especially the role of the 'manager'. This will be more effective if managers, rather than controlling, are seen as supportive of people who are able to manage their own learning.

- HRD relies on some fundamental processes and tools as instruments of the learning process. These include appraisal and personal development planning processes which they need to ensure are seen to add value and achieve their goals.

- Induction and knowledge management are two other processes that should not be just left to managers – HRD should help to define and coach people to use these.

- A systematic and holistic approach to describing capabilities (or competences) is fundamental to the management of learning processes.

- Feedback is a fundamental learning tool and HRD will want to ensure the best approaches are being used, as well as being wise in the use of development/assessment centres.

- Learning processes need to go beyond one-off events and embrace different modes of learning in order to complete the 'learning cycle'. The four modes of learning – education, training, learning from others, and learning from experience – may all feature in many programmes. Companion volumes in this series deal with the professional methodologies of design, delivery and evaluation techniques – and should be referred to for further help.

■ The application to the learner and transfer of learning to others should be a consistent feature of all programmes.

■ A checklist for the 'Elements of Strategic HRD' is contained in Appendix B and summarises most of the points in this book.

REFERENCES AND FURTHER READING

AMERICAN SOCIETY OF TRAINING AND DEVELOPMENT (2003) *The E Learning Series.* Alexandria, Va, American Society of Training and Development.

CAPLAN J. (2003) *Coaching for the Future.* London, CIPD.

COLLINSON C. *and* PARCELL G. (2001) *Learning to Fly.* Capstone.

DIXON N. (2000) *Common Knowledge: How companies thrive by sharing what they know.* Cambridge, Mass, Harvard Business School Press.

EVANS C. (2003) *Managing for Knowledge: HR's strategic role.* Butterworth Heinemann.

HOPE J. *and* HOPE T. (1995) *Transforming the Bottom Line.* London, Nicholas Brealey.

MALONE S. (2003) *Learning about Learning.* London, CIPD.

MEGGINSON D. *and* WHITTAKER V. (1996) *Cultivating Self Development.* London, IPD.

MUMFORD A (1997) *How to Choose a Development Method.* Maidenhead, Peter Honey Publications.

PARSLOE E. *and* WRAY M. (2000) *Coaching and Mentoring: Practical methods to improve learning.* London, Kogan Page.

SIDDONS S. (2001) *Developing Your People.* London, CIPD.

SIMMONS D. (2003) *Designing and Delivering Training.* London, CIPD.

SLOMAN M. (2001) *The E Learning Revolution.* London, CIPD.

STARKEY K., TEMPEST S. *and* McKINLAY A. (2004) *How Organisations Learn.* 2nd edn. Thomson.

VAN DAM N. (2003) 'The e-learning fieldbook'. *Higher Education.*

www.peterhoney.com

5 ■ CAREER AND CONTINUITY PLANNING

There is a wider aspect to the HRD role than meeting capability needs through programmes. Sometimes wrongly separated as a different function, the management of succession and careers is intimately tied up with capability growth, and they belong together. The task in human capital management is to maximise the current *and* future contribution of the people available to us. We can be certain that people are concerned about their own futures, even though they may have different levels of ambition, and we need to respond to that.

Figure 5.1 An overview of tools and processes in career management

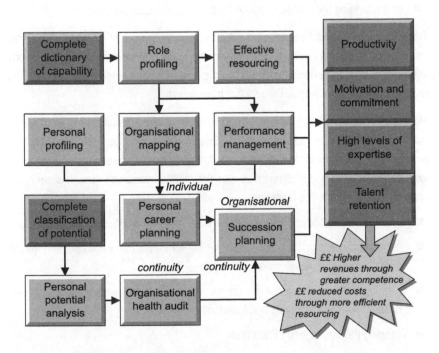

We have used the expression 'continuity' rather than 'succession planning' because this lacks the restrictions of specific jobs and implies a broader approach.

Porras and Collins, in *Built to Last* (1994), found that one of the characteristics of their consistently successful companies was internal promotion. In 1700 years of corporate history of the best companies only four occasions were found of hiring an external CEO. A long way from today's normal practice ...

There are many important decisions to be taken in terms of processes and involvement in this area. Figure 5.1 shows how various processes are linked together, leading to real business benefits. The two key tools are a 'capability dictionary' and a 'classification of potential'. The first has been examined in the previous chapter – here we will look at the issue of potential, and the processes that follow from it.

The people we have, and their future, must all be placed against a background of resourcing needs.

FUTURE RESOURCING

Resource and continuity planning has two aspects:

- looking at what future requirements we might have
- understanding the human resource flows inherent in our organisation.

Figure 5.2 shows the influences on the future requirements – do we need to plan for *more or less* of certain positions, and do we need to plan for any *new* kinds of position? We shall then need to decide whether we can resource them by planned development of people we have, or whether we recruit from outside.

Human resource flow analysis is essential to show us the adequacy or inadequacy of our future resources in general. It takes time to develop people. Have we the raw material to grow the managerial responsibility and technical/professional leadership we need to maintain our competitive position and/or meet our growth plans? Our analysis would include the following:

- mapping demographics, by function, division, location, staff category, and so on
- tracing losses by staff category, and reasons for losses (the most common reason is lack of career or development challenge)
- mapping patterns of career movement – average time in post, typical career 'bridges' between functions and locations
- mapping the distribution of potential

Figure 5.2 Future Resourcing

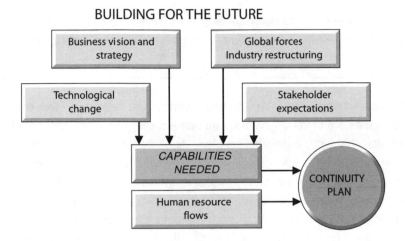

- relating the above to the growth plans of the organisation

- mapping competency distributions within staff groups, as desired at points in the future and compared with today.

These analyses can yield a number of outcomes:

- forecasting future flows both out from, into, and within the organisation

- consequent decisions about young entrant recruitment; actions to reduce attrition in some areas

- planning accelerated development for some individuals

- strengthening of areas that are weak in potential and succession

- taking action on retention of key and potential staff

- creating new career paths

- planning significant capability shifts (and preparing for them).

These outcomes will guide plans and activities for development, and may require some education or training solutions for their achievement.

APPLICATION

What does your organisation know about its future needs? What analyses or human resource flows are done? How often and by whom? How is HRD involved?

Young entrant recruitment is a particularly important area for strategic decisions. It is amazing how short term organisations are here – deciding how many *they can afford* each year. It is not as if the costs are great; this is the tyranny of headcount control. Young entrants, other than those specifically recruited for a here-and-now job, are joining with the future in mind. The number needed is a projection of the resourcing need in 5–20 years time, taking account of losses *en route*, and for a particular set of roles, both managerial and professional. Organisations that take this seriously – such as the major consultancies – not only plan their numbers carefully, but are also extremely clear about what they seek in the candidates. There is no business logic in deciding how many young entrants should be employed based on this year's progress against budget, and even less on headcount targets. Investments in people need different decision parameters than mere expenditure.

Despite the immense growth of HR information systems, the majority of organisations still lack the data with which to do these studies. Data that they had may have been lost through repeated restructuring and systems change. How many HRD functions today do serious long-term human resource planning?

How shall we manage the recruitment and development of young people?

The variation in young entrants today no longer justifies organisations talking about 'graduates' as if they were a homogeneous group. Tertiary education is now available to so many more people that the range of 'qualified young entrants' is very broad. The range of positions for which they can be employed is broad too. Some are hired just to do a job. Others are hired specifically to provide the future leadership of the company. Job titles of those responsible for young entrant recruitment and development (it is recommended they are combined) should reflect this diversity.

Questions for HRD are:

- What range of qualified people do we need, and for what?
- What approaches shall we use for recruitment and selection?

- Shall we manage all or part of the recruitment task centrally?

- Shall we keep any central involvement after induction?

- What induction, training and development shall we offer?

- Shall we create different development tracks?

- Shall we arrange mentors?

- How shall we manage work experiences?

- How shall we help with further professional qualifications?

- To what extent shall we create special relationships with certain institutions and what will be the nature of that relationship?

Surveys of graduates repeatedly show that training schemes feature strongly in their choices of organisation. Exxon Mobil for example has for several years worked in partnership with the London Business School in providing nine modules over three years to new graduates. Many say this influenced their decision to join the company. The erstwhile very successful Kingfisher Management Development Scheme for carefully selected high-quality graduates had a relationship with Templeton College, Oxford, and had a remarkably low loss rate. In contrast, the high attrition experienced by many is often due to unfulfilled expectations.

It is a myth to say that high graduate losses are inevitable because all young people want to experience different organisations early in their career. The best managed

▷ Table 5.1 A policy matrix for young entrant recruitment and development

Type of young entrant	Target positions	Recruit-ment methods	Selection methods	Remuner-ation policy	Training schemes

PhD
MBA
Specialist
Masters
High-quality
  first degree
Typical degree
Lower tertiary
  qualification
School-leaving
  qualifications					

schemes – including early challenging appointments, and constant closeness to how the young people are feeling – bear this out.

Table 5.1 shows a matrix that can be built up. It is sometimes surprising when firms insist that every person must go through the same procedures, however obviously suitable they are, and allow their remuneration systems to eliminate the best people. If it is people that make the difference, surely there can be no other strategy in recruitment than to *try* to get the best possible candidates.

APPLICATION

How do you rate your success in the market in attracting and retaining good-quality young entrants? Draw up the matrix in Table 5.1 for your organisation. Do you feel you differentiate sufficiently in the various columns? What might you change?

CLASSIFYING AND ASSESSING POTENTIAL AND 'TALENT'

'Talent' is a word much used by HR professionals – a good and inclusive word potentially, but often used as a substitute for that very small group that are seen as future senior managers.

Figure 5.3 shows three possible dimensions of potential, which are likely to cover a much greater proportion of the population. 'Height' is about the traditional high flyers. 'Depth' is about creating world-class expertise in core competences, the potential to deepen knowledge and eventually provide technical leadership. 'Breadth' recognises the value from individuals who can turn their hands to several different kinds of job – 'lateral' potential.

Classification

Shell (and others) utilise a very helpful term: CPP – Current Perception of Potential. This recognition that any potential classification is only a perception at a point in time makes it much easier to have a dialogue around it. In choosing classifications, options for describing 'height' include:

- an assessment of *speed* of rising responsibility (eg, two levels within four years)
- an assessment of *levels* beyond the current one (eg, able to rise two levels)
- an estimate of the person's *ceiling* (eg, will make Grade 15).

Figure 5.3 Three Dimensions of Potential

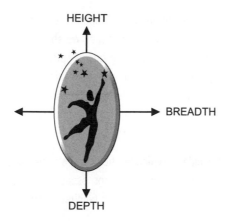

We shall want a broader classification if we take the extended view of talent. Here is the classification used by a young software company:

M1 = able to progress to a senior management position within three years

M2 = able to progress to take management responsibility

TP = able to progress to a leadership role (not necessarily managing people) in his/her technological or professional expertise

L = able to progress laterally and learn new skills outside of his/her current job

O = likely to stay in present job at present level, and develop with the job

E = ability not suited to the current position and level.

Once the system is agreed, the HRD director must decide who will be classified. Will it be everybody? Or just above a certain grade? The question is – why would you not want to apply it to everybody? Talent may lurk in unexpected quarters. Besides, it will be very useful to know the distribution of talent for the population as a whole – and where strong and weak pockets currently exist.

APPLICATION

What system of classification are you using? What percentage of people falls into each classification? What does this tell you about strong and weak pockets?

Assessment

One of the key beliefs we mentioned in Chapter 2 was about potential – are we interested in everyone or just a few? If the former, we shall want to provide a means of assessment for every individual. There is a range of options open to help us – from the simplest of 'managerial judgement' on the appraisal form to sophisticated assessment processes. As always, we do not need the latter if the answer is fairly obvious. But generally more than one judgement, apart from that of the person themselves and their ambition, is desirable.

The HRD director must decide on which methods will be used, and for whom. Figure 5.4 shows a matrix of the options available for assessing potential. In general, the methods in the top left-hand box, if carefully facilitated, should always be the major ones used.

'Ranking' – putting a group of employees at the same level in a ranked order of value – is popular with many companies, but runs the common risk of confusing performance with potential. Performance is about the current job – potential is about something bigger or broader and requiring a different set of capabilities.

Figure 5.4 Options for Assessing potential

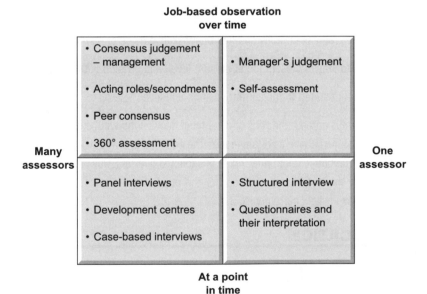

HRD directors and trainers are often asked to comment on the potential of training course participants. There are good reasons to refuse to do this. Participation in a training course is no indicator of how people perform in a job situation – indeed the learning environment should be one where people can experiment and behave differently.

The arguments for being open or otherwise about potential were enumerated in Chapter 2. The most important element in any classification of potential is to recognise that it is *at a point in time*. It needs revisiting regularly, as people change and develop. This transience and opportunity for revisiting makes an easy platform for being open and transparent with people about the perceptions currently held. Thus dialogues about the future should commence 'as we see it at this point in time with the current knowledge available to us'.

If the capability framework is comprehensive and widely understood then dialogue about the future is made much easier. We can focus on 'what it will take to reach your aspirations' rather than an argument about perceptions. We should not assume that it is the job of line managers to have the discussions, which are often difficult for them. Many more junior managers lack the personal maturity to advise beyond a narrow horizon. A good person perhaps to have this dialogue might be the 'grandparent' in a hierarchy – a much more helpful role than being a cursory signatory on an appraisal. Another option is to use third parties such as designated mentors and coaches, HR/HRD staff, or external coaches and advisers.

BALANCED CAREER MANAGEMENT PROCESSES

The task in career management is threefold:

1   to understand the organisation's needs for future capability, and to know what talent it has available to it

2   to provide, as far as possible, a career challenge to individuals that helps them meet their aspirations

3   to provide a means of dialogue between the two.

Figure 5.5, developed by Dr Tony Buley, illustrates these processes and how they interact. On the right-hand side are activities done by an organisation; on the left by the individual – with or without organisational help. It is usually the annual development discussion that brings them together – leading to actions and outputs. When all this works well, nobody should be leaving because they were unsure of the opportunities available. Unfortunately the 'dialogue' is often lacking.

HRD must decide the extent of the provision for employees to explore their options in, for example, career counselling and planning workshops. Organisations that believe strongly in mutual support in career management (eg, Sun Microsystems, Hewlett

Figure 5.5 Processes in continuity and career management

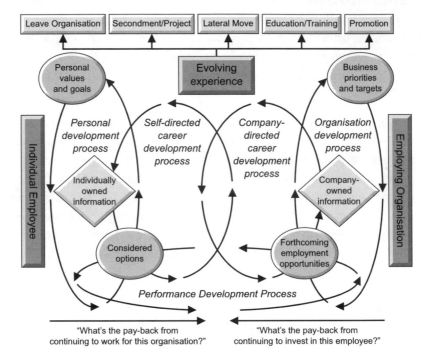

Packard) combine an opportunity for assessment with a number of other dialogues and analytical tools about personal motivations and aspirations. One tool that will benefit everybody is the concept of the 'organisational map'.

MAPPING THE OPPORTUNITIES IN AN ORGANISATION

We know that most development comes through experience, work situations and taking actions ourselves. A manager and an employee can work together to maximise this from a current job. But what about *beyond* the current job? If the organisation wants me to 'manage my own career', I cannot do this without information.

Personal career planning should look towards an 'aiming point' which is beyond the next position, say five to seven years ahead. Organisational mapping is about understanding the opportunities that the organisation can provide in the big picture. Maps help us to navigate; to see where easy crossings over organisational boundaries can be made, and where possible 'high' passes cannot be negotiated. Roads show us the commonly travelled routes. Job profiles on the map enable the highlighting of specific learning opportunities. The good map enables us to be able to answer questions such as the following:

- What kinds of jobs exist in the organisation? (Note this is not the same as the constantly changing organisation chart. It is about the types of job available and their levels of responsibility – these do not change that much. But the map still requires regular maintenance.)

- What are the capability profiles of different types of job in the organisation? (So one can compare their current personal profile with what is needed.)

- Where can one get specialised experience such as man-management, strategic thinking, project management, international, customer-facing, etc?

- What are the typically 'easy' boundary-crossing 'bridges'? (For example from manufacturing management to HR, or finance to strategic planning.)

- What positions do we have that could be classified as 'development posts', ie an able individual could make a positive contribution to the role within three months without prior technical or professional know-how? (These should never be blocked.)

- Where do we have task forces or committees that people could join or that require representatives on external bodies?

From each type of job we can specify typical positions that lead *to* it, and to which *it* leads for the next step. It is not difficult to computerise such a map to be available to all for navigation – or career planning. But at least the HRD director should have it!

APPLICATION

If you do not already have the answers to the above questions in your organisation, try obtaining them.

SOME QUESTIONS IN 'CONTINUITY MANAGEMENT'

Managing and maximising human capital must include the *proactive* development of the talent we have, in addition to the need to manage risk by assessing the levels of continuity that we have. Management looks to HRD to recommend the process to be used. Some of the choices to be made are:

- *Do we want to identify successors for specific posts, or create 'pools' of people available for similar types of position'?* Pools are more flexible, and provide a more reliable picture of continuity strength. Nevertheless, there will be some critical and unique positions for which named successors will be sought. So our continuity plan will probably contain both. Organisations are generally focused on management when it comes to succession planning. However, increasingly the depth of specialist expertise and technical/professional leadership is a major factor in competitive advantage.

- *How far ahead do we want to look?* One of the more useful 'markers' to apply to current incumbents is EDM (earliest date for move) – that is, the earliest date at which the individual should be considered for his or her next career move. In continuity planning, we want to have (a) an option for the unexpected and (b) an option ready at the time of the incumbent's 'EDM'. Figure 5.6 shows the different horizons relevant to continuity planning.

- *What information do we need; how shall we obtain and review it?* HR tends to over-engineer the information needed. We should work with the minimum required to trigger actions; backup data can be obtained as needed. Such minimal information will include date of birth, date of starting the current job, performance and potential ratings, and mobility.

For acquiring and reviewing the information there are many options. HQ staff can tour the organisation asking the relevant people for their views. Local management teams can submit forms and papers. HR can manage it through their own hierarchy and network. Annual meetings of succession planning subcommittees can take place, resourced by an HR secretariat.

An approach developed by ICL, now Fujitsu Systems, and subsequently widely adopted, is one that integrates succession discussions with operational business reviews.

Figure 5.6 Succession horizons

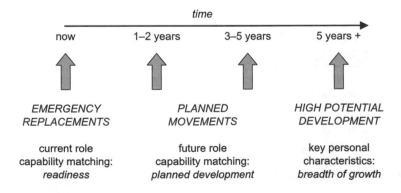

		time →	
now	1–2 years	3–5 years	5 years +
EMERGENCY REPLACEMENTS	*PLANNED MOVEMENTS*		*HIGH POTENTIAL DEVELOPMENT*
current role capability matching: *readiness*	future role capability matching: *planned development*		key personal characteristics: *breadth of growth*

Generally termed the organisational and management review (OMR) (or similar) it synchronises a formal review of issues such as succession, key people development, strategic training issues, and potential strength with the cycle of business reviews. Typically this might take place every four to six months, being 'cascaded upwards' through business units and subsidiary companies, eventually reaching the CEO. Each level in the cascade generates information that feeds into the next level.

This approach puts the ownership with line management, links business performance with people capability, recognises the dynamism of organisational and people development, and provides continually updated succession information. Actions to close gaps or deal with problems can be taken regularly.

- *Do we want to look only internally?* Some have created a 'shadow succession plan,' ie where people are not available inside the organisation, who is there outside who might be earmarked for hiring (or trying to hire) should the need arise? This cuts out considerable time from the search process.

A 'partner' search consultant who knows the organisation well is needed for this. It is not easy to do, (although its merits are clear) and is probably worth doing for only a small number of key positions.

CHOICES IN MANAGING CAREER DEVELOPMENT

Do we want any 'high flyer programmes', and if so how shall we position them?

Many organisations were very reluctant to indicate either to individuals or to the organisation at large that some people are on 'accelerated development', or a designated 'high potential' scheme. With the growth of 'talent management', this reluctance has lessened. We have argued earlier for a policy of openness. However, overt 'labelling' is best avoided as much as is feasible. One large international company describes its development programme for the few as 'career broadening'. another calls its high potential assessment centres 'career guidance', and every attendee receives the same feedback and guidance regardless of whether their career path is seen as towards general management.

One policy decision for such schemes is 'nomination' vs 'application'. The choice relates to the general beliefs and values of the organisation; however, if these wish to reflect openness and personal ownership then application must be allowed. This can be balanced by controlled *acceptance* – through entry standards and careful counselling.

In career development, how do we want to balance specialist vs generalist development?

In many national and corporate cultures, development is 'silo driven' right up to high levels. This creates a problem in the lack of overview that senior people have. Others decide deliberately the points at which people should gain experience of another function. Some have no specific policy, and just let careers develop opportunistically. Some of the different models employed may be summarised as follows:

- *The Narrow 'T'.* In this model people remain specialists until the highest level, managing groups of their own specialism but not working outside it. It is not until the top of the 'tree' that they take broader collegiate responsibilities (typical of Germany).

- *The Wide 'T'.* This is a more common model in the UK where, beyond say the first 10 years of specialism and junior management, people broaden across functional boundaries and become a 'management resource' thereafter.

- *The 'I'.* Here young entrants are given a general knowledge of the organisation and its business for perhaps up to three years. They then specialise in a chosen area, and remain in that area until reaching senior management, when they become more general again.

- *The 'double 'T'.* Starting as specialists, people are broadened through a variety of jobs and then follow the above pattern.

- *The 'Y' model.* Found in highly technical organisations, career opportunities and matching rewards exist to a more or less equally high level for both specialists and generalists.

APPLICATION

Which models are deployed deliberately, or implicitly, in your organisation? Do they meet the needs of how the organisation plans to develop strategically? If change would be helpful, what would be required to achieve it?

This is an important policy decision that has to be matched with rewards and which clearly influences people's ability to manage their own careers. One symptom of a problem is where good specialists become poor generalists because there is no alternative route for progress. If the organisation believes in the value of some varied experience, then it has to facilitate the movement across boundaries that is needed – some of which are not easy to 'self-manage'. SmithKlineBeecham, for example, had a policy of '2 functions plus 2 countries plus 2 business units' for future general managers. Achieving this requires some planned career management, but at least the goal is clear.

The question to be answered as always is, 'What mix of general/specialist experience will best serve the strategy of the organisation?' Most organisations today need expertise in their core competencies that is at least as critical a contributor as management capability.

How do we want to balance internal promotion vs external hire?

In order to be effective at human resource planning, the planned ratio of internal promotion to external hire is critical. It will be different depending on levels, and possibly on job groups also. Many of the 'Built to Last' companies mentioned earlier never recruit, unless in exceptional circumstances, beyond graduate level. They take more than they need at that point in order to allow for controlled attrition.

Others have a deliberate policy to bring in new blood constantly, and every vacancy is competed for on equal terms by internal and external candidates. But many would state a deliberate desire to give *first* choice to their own people, while making it clear that they will go outside when necessary.

Many managers seem convinced that the world outside is full of better people than they have, even though, to their surprise, their own people leave and do much better. When we see that happening, there may be a lesson to be learnt about our own development processes.

Few have a planned ratio that is built around their strategic needs and to which they seek to work. However, there is much value in having such a ratio, especially in providing a target and standard for development activities.

APPLICATION

In the various parts of your organisation what have been the historical ratios in resourcing at different levels? How many of these have been the result of a deliberate policy? How do they relate to loss rates and reasons for leaving? Do you draw any conclusions about whether a more planned approach would be of benefit?

Vacancy management – what access shall we give to opportunities?

Here there may be a dilemma between *open access* to jobs and *planned development*, where the two might be seen to be in conflict. It is a key *policy* decision as to which jobs will be openly advertised. In general, in the public sector it is the norm for this to be done for all; practice in the private sector varies enormously. Some companies do so only when all else has failed; others make it a norm for all but the most senior posts. If an organisation is preaching personal career ownership, then it seems inconsistent if people do not then have the opportunity to apply for jobs openly. The ability of managers to block applications from their staff need to be controlled too.

The dilemma can be resolved by maintaining open access, and ensuring that those for whom the job is planned apply for it and are considered competitively. Alternatively the policy can be clear that 'where jobs have planned successors they will not be advertised'.

The advent of organisational intranets and webpages has encouraged the use of them for advertising internal vacancies, and this increases the availability of such information, especially across boundaries. Sun Microsystems, for example, advertises every job in the world (other than the three top levels) to every site, and anyone can make an application (electronically, of course).

Whatever is done has to have credibility, and not be seen to be a showcase behind which selection is fixed. The more 'shared' the information about aspirations and perceived potential, the easier it is to have coherence between the planned and the open.

Using secondments for development

Secondments are one of the most valuable forms of development, and are essential in 'flatter' organisations. Relatively low risk to all parties, they provide the opportunity for new learning through real-life experiences. This has been the traditional route for international assignments, and many organisations have deployed them on a broader basis – to project teams, to new departments, or from line to staff posts and vice versa. Hertfordshire County Council is one organisation that, in an effort to counter fewer traditional career opportunities, introduced a 24-page booklet entitled *Guidelines for Effective Secondments, Job Swaps and Job Shadowing.*

Encouraging or facilitating secondments is a rewarding exercise in people development. It helps to take some central ownership for the process because, with the best will in the world, guarantees made at the beginning of secondment may prove difficult to keep by the originating party (who might have left or been reorganised). It is a sad waste of valuable experience to see returning expatriates with nowhere to go. HRD needs to be closely involved with the 'expatriate' department – and preferably responsible for it. This is one case where firm guidelines and disciplines are needed to help the process.

IN BRIEF

- The first step is in resourcing for the future. This may not be seen as HRD's job – what is important is that it happens. A crystal ball is needed first to see what might change in the requirements for types of job, and the capabilities that go with them. In parallel we need to study the human resource flows of key groups based on history and employee data to see what this tells us about future needs.

- One of the key resourcing areas is our strategy for recruiting and developing young entrants. Far more diverse than just 'graduates', this requires a number of key questions to be answered.

- Along with the capability framework, the second key tool is a classification of potential and a strategy for assessing it. Decisions have to be made about how far down the organisation this will be applied. We suggested three dimensions of potential – height, depth and breadth.

- Three types of process need to come together for career management – those done by the organisation in resource planning and potential assessment, individual career planning, and dialogue between the two.

- A number of questions present themselves about the information we need and how it will be maintained, vacancy management, career paths and secondments. They are all crucial to the growth of human capital through vital experience.

REFERENCES AND FURTHER READING

BEAZLEY H., BOENSISCH J. *and* HARDEN D. (2002) *Continuity Management.* John Wiley.

MAYO A.J. (1991) *Managing Careers: Strategies for organisations.* London, IPM.

McCALL M. Jr, LOMBARDO M. *and* MORRISON A. (1998) *The Lessons of Experience.* Lexington Books.

MUMFORD A. (1980) *Making Experience Pay.* McGraw Hill.

PEIPER I.M., ARTHUR M., GOFFEE R. *and* MORRIS T. (1999) *Career Frontiers.* Oxford, Oxford University Press.

PORRAS J.I. *and* COLLINS J.C. (1994) *Built to Last.* New York, Harpers Press.

SADLER P. (1993) *Managing Talent.* Economist Books.

WILLIAMS M. (2000) *The War for Talent: Getting the best from the best.* London, CIPD.

6 ■ PRIORITISING AND RESOURCING

As we collect together all the demands on our resources from the drivers described in the earlier chapters, we could be justified in arguing that *all* should be met since they are all business driven. Nevertheless, some activities are more critical than others, and some have a clearer and stronger return on investment (RoI). In reality too, most HRD directors will have a budget and limited resources. Prioritising must be done, and optimal resources chosen.

The demands on our resources will not just be for programmes. They will also be for new or redesigned *policies* and *processes*, and for consultant and coaching efforts helping managers and teams to be better at learning.

PRIORITISING THE DEMANDS

Prioritising of new initiatives is always a balancing act. Should first priority be given to all those learning programmes aimed at increasing the current year's bottom line? Should HRD focus on what it knows it is good at (or likes doing)? Longer-term development is more about ongoing consistent investment in processes (the only major cost being in the dedicated and intelligent time/effort of a small number of professionals plus that contributed by line managers), whereas training is more diverse. Of course, like other good things in life, much learning comes 'free' — if only we can harness it.

Accountants work in yearly cycles (mostly). Life is not like that, however. If we are to respond to business needs we need to maintain the planned learning needs, but at the same time be able to respond to those that emerge during the year (such as a merger or a new piece of legislation or a major competitive threat). We need systems and guidelines for making choices — both at the end of formal needs analysis and in

Figure 6.1 Classifying priorities

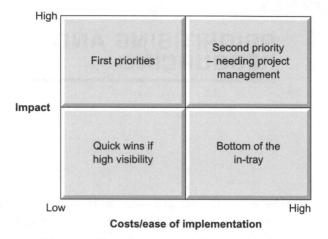

weighing up new priorities. It is too easy, in the eagerness to be wanted and to please others, to say 'yes' to every request that comes in or results from legitimate consultancy activity. Remember from Chapter 1 – strategy is as much about saying 'no, we won't do that' as it is saying 'yes, of course'. Any freelance consultant knows this dilemma well!

Figure 6.1 shows a commonly used matrix for determining priorities. It is used to place various potential initiatives on two dimensions – that of the impact on the organisation versus the ease and cost of implementation. By 'impact' we mean the effect it will have on the drivers outlined in Chapters 1 and 2, and this will be a combination of *speed* and *effect* on what is important. As we discuss in Chapter 8, there are several 'bottom lines' that we might be impacting – financial, strategic or adding value to a key stakeholder.

The techniques in that chapter should be used to assess impact. High impact, high cost means it is no less important, but is going to need more attention, and initiatives here will probably be project managed over time, but started as soon as possible. We should also look carefully at alternative methods of delivery – can we reduce the cost by using more of our own resources, by having fewer off-the-job elements, and so on? Low impact/low cost should not be ignored – sometimes for political or marketing reasons we may want to do some things here, but they should be strictly controlled.

Priority diagrams can be drawn separately for different groups of initiatives – for example, programmes for different populations, policies and processes, and consultant work. One might have a dozen or so of them to help visualise how the real priorities are distributed. These pictures will give us a sense of balance of our efforts across the organisation, and as directed at organisational, team and individual learning.

HRD's agenda vs the organisation's needs – a note of caution

Few HRD directors will say other than that they do their best to focus on the organisation's needs. However, in practice this may mean they decide, *in best faith*, what they believe is right for it. That belief is inevitably conditioned by where they come from personally. HRD has a significant share of idealist relationship-oriented trainers who are quite lost when it comes to business issues, and who believe that the problem for their organisation is that it is *over* task oriented and insufficiently *people* oriented. They also have their own personal interests in the learning arena and love to practise them on the people in their organisation. If our model for creating a strategy is followed, this should not be the case – but when setting priorities HRD needs to be very objective. For this reason we recommend in the next chapter that a steering group, or similar body, should make the final priority decisions.

Priority setting is not an exact science – it is also pragmatic and political. We do not like to say 'no' to requests, even if clearly not a good use of our resource, especially if we see a longer-term relationship at stake or an entry point into a previously difficult area. But a systematic starting point is the mark of the professional.

APPLICATION

If you take each population in your organisation and plot what you are currently doing on a matrix such as Figure 6.1, what does it look like? How balanced is it? Do the same for the work that is going on with policies and processes.

Now look at the balance of effort that is going towards organisational, team and individual learning.

Does that feel 'healthy'? The test is, 'How comfortable would I be displaying this analysis to the board?'

FUNDING STRATEGIES

It is fine to say 'most learning is free' but, however true that is, we still need funds for:

- professional HRD management and staff
- subcontracted professional help
- equipment and facilities, our own or those bought in
- learning materials
- IT support.

▷ Table 6.1 Funding mechanisms for HRD

Mode of funding	Advantages	Disadvantages
1 Centrally funded as an overhead cost; resources cut to that budget and events provided free to users	■ stability, clarity, ease of planning ■ message of importance of training and development ■ not subject to 'client' unit budget difficulties	■ no ownership by units, ■ so use of events may not be taken seriously ■ central focus may not meet the real needs ■ risk of complacency by HRD ■ all funds in 'one basket'
2 Funded through negotiated annual contributions from units	■ relatively stable for planning purposes ■ units have ownership of their budget ■ opportunity to create internal client relationships	■ assumes the nature of demand does not change through the year – difficult to be responsive ■ may be at risk of renegotiation, especially when restructuring takes place ■ time wasted in negotiations
3 Combination of (1) and (2) with a 'central subsidy' (for strategic programmes and/or making the use of internal resources attractive financially)	■ combines the advantages of (1) and (2) ■ judicious application of central subsidies enables priorities to be given to strategic change and cross-organisational issues	■ has some of the disadvantages of (1) and (2), but to a lesser extent
4 Free market approach – departments contract event by event and pay the advertised price	■ able to be really responsive to the needs of units ■ no scope for HRD to 'peddle their own agenda'	■ a lot of time is spent in selling and negotiating ■ no ability to plan resources – so will keep in-house to a minimum ■ 'numbers' overtake quality ■ difficult to give any cohesive messages across all the organisation ■ become a supplier rather than a support for the strategies

In the next chapter we look at some of the strategies for achieving the desired funds. Normally they will have to be found internally, but – depending on the nature of our organisation and where it is located – we may be able to secure funds from external bodies such as (in the UK) Learning and Skills Councils, European Union funds, or other Government initiatives. Sometimes the bureaucracy involved in achieving such funds outweighs the financial gain, but each organisation has to decide for itself.

Internal funding

Internal funding is a very political matter, and the HRD director will be subject to organisational accounting rules. Table 6.1 provides some options and their effects.

The basic positions vary, as shown in the table. As you go from position 1 to 4 it becomes more and more difficult to be 'strategic' and HRD becomes progressively more involved in daily planning and number balancing. On the other hand, if HRD is a central service, and the organisation is very much devolved, with business units being very different and the level of cross-organisational synergy very low, it can be a very appropriate model.

Option 3 has a lot to be said for it. It enables a balance between strategic priorities to be maintained and yet for most units can see that learning is a necessary and *essential* cost of operating. The full market position (option 4), though popular, has significant disadvantages, as the pricing will have to fund the HRD overheads and activities for the benefit of the organisation as a whole. Accountants like to distribute costs out to profit centres and have the minimal in the 'centre' – which is fine for their book-keeping but usually wrong for the organisational strategy. You cannot expect units to financially support initiatives they have no local interest in, and simultaneously be pushed for better results.

One critical factor in the funding equation is the freedom given to units to use external suppliers as against the internal option. In some organisations this freedom is zero – if an internal option is there it should be used. In others, the freedom to make a choice between alternatives is total. The problem of the latter is that there is a strange psychological tendency for units to believe the grass is greener externally, and to reject an internal option just because it is internal. Rationality may not rule!

Budgeting

Organisations budget in many ways and HRD has to fit in with the standard process used. The annual ritual is discredited and a number of companies are exploring other approaches – a website devoted to this is included in References and Further Reading.

Alternative approaches are:

- incremental budgeting – an increment based on last year
- fixed budget – remains more or less the same year on year
- variable budget – linked to parameters such as headcount
- zero-based budget – built up from the actual needs year on year
- rolling budget – reviewed quarterly in the light of requirements and business performance.

In HRD a combination of either variable or zero-based – for the ongoing activities – and the rolling budget to provide flexibility and responsiveness is ideal.

Pricing

Sources of funds are one thing, but how those funds are allocated to activities is another. Pricing is a strategic tool itself; and some options are shown in Table 6.2.

The first question is whether HRD or the training department is expected to make an internal profit, or to subsidise some activities from others. Internal profit-making is

▶ Table 6.2 Pricing options

Pricing approach	Objective	Comments
1 Standard training day rate	Simplicity, volume, 'bums on seats'	Focus is on cost rather than value; training as a commodity
2 Activity-based cost price	Reflect true costs of development and delivery	This is better, but problem of forecasting product life for development recovery; also more work involved
3 Consultancy-based price, at cost	Straight no-frills internal price	Value of offering may not be appreciated
4 Consultancy-based price, at market rate less discount(s)	Demonstrate both true value and benefit of internal customer	Gives flexibility to control messages
5 Consultancy-based price, at market rate	Demonstrate value of solution offered and awareness of market	Places HRD firmly in competitive market

generally not recommended. It is an unnecessary source of conflict and game playing, and adds no value to the organisation or its customers. Subsidising low-price or free activities from high-price ones may sometimes be helpful – for example pump priming a network, sponsoring some internal departmental development or handling some unbudgeted but important need. However, although pragmatic, this is not ideal, and it is better to have specifically reserved funds in the budget for such needs.

There will always be a portfolio of 'standard' courses, and these can be priced on a standard basis. The key parameter in such pricing will be 'lecturer productivity'.

The ratio of these to 'nonstandard', 'one-off', pilot or bespoke events will vary between organisations. If HRD has decided to run itself as a consultancy then it will have standard fee rates per person as a basis of costing. These fee rates will be the person's salary marked up for the actual overhead costs of running the HRD department – nonrevenue-earning days, management, premises, marketing and support staff. These should be allocated on an activity-based costing method, and may typically double the all-in salary cost.

Some events may be 'free' to all participants, as they are centrally funded. (The most common approach here is that individual units pay for travel and accommodation only. This tends to disadvantage poorer units or units at a long distance, so they may need to be subsidised.) Typical centrally funded initiatives would be high potential development centres and educational programmes, senior management development, change management programmes and graduate development.

Pricing strategies 3, 4 and 5 in Table 6.2 show different ways of pricing for consultancy. Just to do it at cost should certainly give a cheaper option to the client unit than an external proposal. To price at market rate means being market competitive and making profit. One might do this for proposals that are not firmly in HRD's 'added value portfolio' and, although preferring to say 'no', client relations indicate that this would cause the relationship to suffer.

Strategy 4 has merit. Pricing by value, ie market rate, enables the client unit sees the true market cost. This can then be discounted – say by 20–25 per cent – which would bring it down to cost as a standard 'internal discount'. Various subsidies can be applied – up to 100 per cent – if it can be paid for out of 'strategic funding'.

APPLICATION

Examine your funding and pricing strategies against the alternatives given. Could you see any merit in alternative approaches? Who would benefit and how? Be sure that, overall, the organisation would gain, rather than just HRD!

Funding through external revenue generation

Many organisations today have a policy of minimal self-owned infrastructure for learning and development. Depending on what we have, there may be opportunities for external revenues from:

- *letting out facilities and/or equipment.* This utilises spare capacity and maximises the return on fixed costs.

- *selling places on internal training courses.* This is commonly done on technical courses, where know-how is the main learning goal, or on routine skills courses. It is inappropriate for events where open discussion on the organisation is needed.

- *providing external client consultancy.* This utilises spare capacity of learning consultants or trainers on external client opportunities.

- *licensing training methodologies or selling materials.* This can be done where these are not deemed to be of competitive advantage.

- providing HRD services to other organisations.

Some of these activities are very attractive to managers and staff, as well as to senior management for the resource productivity they bring. They enable entrepreneurialism without risk. There are many potential advantages to those involved:

- sharpening consultancy skills in a commercial environment

- learning business skills firsthand

- keeping an external focus.

The danger is clear, however – people whose prime task is to meet the needs of the *organisation* get more fun from working externally. It develops them personally, gives them pride in generating revenue, and keeps them from the daily politics and trials of organisational life. Furthermore, when successful, management sets revenue targets, linked to bonuses, and this activity dominates priorities. My own experience in this area has led me to the following conclusion – if there is good potential for external revenue to be made from training activities, one should keep the resources involved as far as is feasible separate from those dedicated to internal learning.

Many companies have realised that they have created some internal excellence in some training areas and this may be of interest to other organisations – first to existing customers but then going beyond that. Most of the IT companies have external training organisations – specialising in IT areas, but branching out into others too. ICL named its training business 'Peritas' with a very broad remit; this eventually became 'KnowledgePool', which was sold off and is a very successful training company at the time of writing; British Airways spun out its 'Speedwing Training' after its success in its own quality service programme. Another example is the small Bedfordshire company, Duttons Engineering – which, after some years of highly focused and successful training, created a division called 'Business Excellence Training', 'committed to the provision of high quality training which will enable organisations to achieve excellence by realising the potential of their people'.

Where both external and internal exist, staff can move between each 'side' (because the advantages outlined above are real and worthwhile), but should not be asked to serve two masters at one time – the needs of the organisation will lose out. However, because of the advantages of external exposure one might allow, say, up to 5 to 10 days external work per annum.

PREMISES, EQUIPMENT AND TECHNOLOGY

Many well-known organisations have maintained large centralised training establishments, some with grand names, although this is far less common after the downturns following 2001. Many have seen them as a luxury or as inconsistent with the core businesses of the organisation, and have sold them off to become specialist conference or hospitality centres.

They can serve many purposes in addition to their main function, which is to provide an environment for training to take place. They bring people together from different parts of the organisation, are used for different types of meetings, corporate celebrations or rituals. They become an integral part both of the culture and the defining of the culture.

It is likely that the decision to acquire, maintain or sell such a centre will not be in the hands of the HRD director. However, they will certainly have a strong interest in it, and it will significantly affect the job they do. What factors govern such a decision?

- *the need to have the most cost-effective delivery of training.* We should beware of the trap of believing that because costs are adequately recovered *internally –*

through cross-charging – that therefore the facility is cost-effective. Calculations must take a company-wide view. The considerations to be taken into account include first, those relating to the organisation's own premises (24-7 costs), such as premises costs (rent or ownership costs, utilities, services), equipment purchase and depreciation, catering costs, travel for company delegates, extent of subsidy obtainable through external revenues by allowing others to use the facility, facilities management cost and time, and corporate overhead contribution. Second, those relating to external facilities (as used costs), such as delegate day rates (including all room hire and meals), special equipment hire, travel for company delegates, and travel and accommodation for training staff. One cannot predict any general outcome of such calculations as every organisation's situation will be different. Where a large amount of *standard* training has to be delivered, it is likely that the economics will swing in favour of having a dedicated site. For monitoring purposes, ratios such as 'cost per training day delivered' will provide a suitable measure.

However, costs are not the only factor to be considered. We know that the standard training course is *not* necessarily an effective way of learning, but all central premises will seek to maximise utilisation of facilities and trainers. There is a therefore a desire both to fill the rooms available with courses, but also a natural tendency to 'fit' courses into standard lengths. So many courses become four and a half days long, which may have nothing to do with what is necessary for the learning to take place. One of the advantages of *not* having an owned facility is that this tendency is much reduced, *and* because external costs are so much more visible, there is pressure in the *opposite* direction. The HRD director needs to have overall control of this resource in order to keep the right balance. A good costs comparison, therefore, will bring in factors that reflect these tendencies, and the only way to do this is to 'zero-base' all the training that is done.

APPLICATION

Pick a variety of events that are being currently run as off-the-job programmes. What are their learning objectives? What alternative ways of meeting those objectives could be available? Form a view of the cost/effectiveness balance of the alternatives.

■ *the benefit of people in the organisation learning from each other.* Learning is not just in classrooms but is live and dynamic between people. A common centre is an enabler of learning about other parts of the organisation, of the sharing of good practice, and the making of contacts and networks that will be useful in the future. The social factors of mixing not only within a course but between courses are significant and are hard to quantify.

- *the benefit of having training staff co-located with their place of delivery.* This is a mixed blessing. Clearly there are benefits from the closeness to facilities, for the ability to utilise training staff productively, for being able to create a team and departmental spirit. But these establishments tend to be quite pleasant and relaxed, and provide a very comfortable working environment. This is not a problem in itself of course, but can lead to complacency in staff and a strong vested interest in its continuation.

- *the benefit of a corporate cultural centre as a means of cohesion.* Many a manager and many an employee have a special fondness for their training centre. Full of memories, both social and to do with learning, they may look forward to every visit. The centre may be an environment that provides some escape from the everyday grind, where people from different parts of the company can be met and talked to, and where somehow the spirit of the company can be found. The 'real' culture and values live in the bars and dining tables and leisure facilities of the organisation's training centre. Even the presence of 'paying guests' – external revenue providers – seems not to diminish the sense of ownership that people feel. Accountants do not generally take account of such 'soft' benefits when doing their evaluations. The question of balance is the extent to which this feeling of cohesion is *positive* in promoting the desired culture, or whether it perpetuates an old way of being that is inappropriate for the future.

Corporate 'universities'

During the 1990s there was a tremendous growth in so-called corporate universities, especially in the USA. The European Foundation of Management Development held a seminar in 1997 to study these, and it appeared that many were 'previous training departments with delusions of grandeur'. It became a fashionable term to use for a centralised training and education establishment.

A famous British example is the Unipart Group, championed by John Neill, CEO, in Oxford. The public website in 2004 has a section entitled 'The Learning Organisation', saying:

❝ Unipart Univerity's mission is to develop, train and inspire people to achieve World Class performance within UGC companies and amongst its stakeholders.

The Unipart 'U' is the first area seen by any visitor to the group's head office in Oxford. Opened in 1993, the 'U' is an integral part of working life in Unipart – employees enter the 'U' every day on their way to and from work and learn as well as teach in the facility.

'It reflects our intention to train and inspire people to achieve world-class performance within UGC and its stakeholders,' said John Neill.

The Unipart U has become the platform from which we can see the direction for the future. There's a good commercial argument for it; it's a route to competitive advantage and it enhances shareholder value by preventing our people's skills from becoming obsolete.

Our next stage, The Virtual 'U', a web-based method of delivering course work, personal development plans and performance management via the desktop computer, combines the best aspects of web-learning with the leading edge techniques for knowledge management. 〃

One of the first was the famous Motorola University. This had high status in the company and generated some significant intellectual capital – it was not just a source of courses. In particular, the 'six sigma' approach to process quality was developed there, widely applied today in many companies. At the time of writing the traumas affecting the telecommunications industry caused the University to be first distributed out to the business sectors and then to be considerably reduced – now just focusing on six sigma training. Many others have gone by the wayside, although examples are still to be found. Lloyds TSB has its University, their central learning facility, in Solihull.

In the high-tech industries the term has been used for a centre of dispensing e-learning. Dell, for example, offers an extensive range of courses through Dell University, not only to its own employees but to schools in the USA.

One of the best-known corporate facilities – that of General Electric – is just called GE Crotonville, a 52-acre campus in New York state. This is seen very firmly as a central developer of values and culture. It is well described in Jack Welch's autobiography, and he spent many days a year teaching and debating with managers from all over the world. He saw it as a fundamental platform for communication and common strategic understanding.

An interesting variation is 'Aquas Universitas', or the University of Water, set up by Anglian Water. This is nothing to do with training at all, but is a systematic repository of company knowledge. Senior managers take ownership for 'faculties' and look after the use and growth of knowledge and experience in a designated area.

There is a sense of grandeur about the corporate university which may appeal to some CEOs a lot more than to the employees. In contrast to the 'bricks and mortar' visible to everybody, a *virtual* centre of learning may enjoy some of the benefits of centralisation, at least economically. It loses out on the 'club' aspect, on learning from and with colleagues, but is better able to be customised and 'just-in-time'. It is best not seen as an alternative, but more a potential addition to the learning resources available.

Equipment and technology

Technology has made a tremendous difference to learning as an enabler over the past few years. The first edition of this book in 1998 did not even have e-learning in its index – the term was in its infancy. In the classroom, the combination of multimedia laptops – with online access to the Internet, DVD players, sound and movie clips – and data projection has revolutionised presentation methodology. Learners have the opportunity to contribute and vote answers by wireless simultaneous response receivers, and to interact with one another in virtual discussion. Business schools and corporate universities have set up virtual learning environments (VLEs) – where learners can access materials and interact with teachers, facilitators, coaches and one another.

Expensive hardware that used to be needed for hands-on students – such as cockpit simulators and large computers – can be simulated online, and there is no need for students to be where the hardware is located.

The once-popular Learning Resource Centre is found less and less, as most employees have their own computer access and a range of e-learning options. This was a dedicated space packed with learning materials for employees to use freely. In practice many were rarely used and the costs not recovered in learning benefits.

The use of e-learning

This is an enormous area, but one of the key areas for HRD today – what should we deliver to learners electronically? Since 1992, according to one of its great proponents, Cisco, its use has grown by 300 per cent per annum. A KPMG investigation, in late 2001, using 12 major companies as cases, stated that implementing e-learning could save 'more than £7.5m a year for the average FTSE-250 company'. E-learning costs per head are estimated to be 70 per cent lower than classroom costs.

The market is crowded with thousands of suppliers, many of which are much more focused on content than on the learning process. The opportunities include:

- content options, that can be selected by students into their own learning programme
- online expertise
- opportunity to interact with the material
- colleague collaboration
- communities of sharing
- online coaching
- surveys.

Cisco, one of the major suppliers, offers this advice:

- develop a strong partnership with IT
- integrate e-learning as a strategic element in change and operational plans
- use e-learning to address bottom-up company-wide issues
- don't expect e-learning to replace classroom and other face-to-face events.

The KPMG report outlines many errors that have been made. One contributor said 'for every pound spent on technology, £2 was spent on change management and communications'. Another said 'you can rapidly become humbled when you realise that it's the learning which is important, not the technology'. The report said 'only a third of participants have any form of evaluation in place'. For many companies, e-learning became an end in itself and they lost the perspective of seeing it as a tool of learning. The motivation of students to complete an e-learning course, once started, has become a key issue.

HRD has to have a specific and carefully thought through strategy for the use of e-learning, and be able to answer these questions:

- What e-learning infrastructure should we put in place?
- What e-learning partners should we have?
- What skills do we need in house?
- What parameters shall we use to check whether e-delivery is suitable for all or part of a learning need?
- How shall we equip learners to make maximum use of e-delivery?
- How shall we balance cost considerations with ensuring learning effectiveness?

ORGANISATION, ROLES AND CAPABILITIES

As we showed in Figure 4.2, the HRD function should see itself as the hub of the wheel of people development, with many groups and individuals contributing to success beyond those within a designated department. So the way people development is co-ordinated, recognising all the different contributors, is just as critical as the skills available in HRD itself.

HRD organisation

What does HRD potentially consist of? In this book we have talked about the following:

- organisation development
- leadership and management education/development
- young entrant recruitment and development
- capability training for all populations
- professional qualifications
- career and succession planning
- knowledge management.

In some organisations all these seven may be in separate units, coming together only at the central HR director level. There are a number of questions to be asked at that central level. However, for many readers this may be a given, as HRD comprises only one person or is very small (or is even combined with the broader HR role). Individuals have to embrace a wide variety of activities, and have to be skilled at deciding what should merit their personal attention, what can be outsourced, and that which cannot be resourced at all.

In larger organisations some of the questions that arise are as follows.

To what extent should HRD activities be integrated?

There is a strong argument for all seven of the activities mentioned above to be integrated under one person, even though they may not all report organisationally to that person. In the author's last corporate role as Director of People Development for the ICL Group, all these were brought together, with great benefits in cross-support and in taking an integrated approach to each 'population'. When Tony McCarthy took up the HR reins at the Royal Mail in 2003 with one of the largest transformational challenges of any kind to be undertaken, all these activities were put under one 'Chief Learning

Officer'. If we apply 'client thinking' rather than 'functional thinking', integration is a natural conclusion.

How do we see the total HRD resource across the organisation?

This will reflect organisational structure, culture and values, although HRD is in a unique position to break down rigidity and boundaries, if thought desirable. We may have a central resource dedicated to cross-company programmes and not involved with the day-to-day training and development needs of people and teams. Their prime focus would be on organisational learning, on policy and global processes. Out in the units are the people who run the activities that are needed locally. Every now and then they all meet together and discuss areas of common interest.

This division between central and local has the benefit of dedicated accountability, but can lead to isolation of any part, and duplication between units. The HRD director will always have the challenge of building synergy across the various professional resources.

How should an HRD function interface with business units?

There are three basic options for interfacing:

1   By populations that have *common development needs* across the organisation as a whole. Thus HRD would have staff dedicated to salespeople, management, clerical staff, etc, and their overall needs. If this is chosen, the integrated model makes sense.

2   By organisational unit – for all the staff in one *unit*. This has the advantage of strong client relationships, and the HRD 'relationship manager' can develop a strong affinity for the activities, problems and people of a unit.

3   By *subject* area – organised by skill or expertise, each person or group offers a range of consultancy or events available to all. This would be the structure of the traditional training department, allied to the first option but focused on training.

In practice, a combination of these may be chosen. Thus a person responsible for a subject area may also take the role of relationship manager for one or more units.

Do we want to run primarily as a supplier or as a consultancy?

We cannot avoid doing some of both. Indeed, it is dangerous to see this as black and white, and – for example – to suddenly abandon the course catalogue in an effort to show people a new consultancy mode. 'Customers' may not think as radically as HRD, and have expectations that need time to adjust. Also inevitably there will be some regularly run scheduled events, dealing with core capabilities and continuing skill enhancement needs. But the *primary* choice will radically affect the skills on which we focus, the eventual portfolio of activities, the measures of success and the whole HRD culture. It will result from our conclusions from the questions posed in the previous chapter.

If HRD wishes to position all or part of itself as an internal consultancy, then the disciplines and routines of a consultancy need to be put in place. This will include:

- consultancy skills training
- a commercial structure
- time control disciplines
- utilisation targets
- project management
- resource allocation.

APPLICATION

Consider the HRD organisational structure of which you are part. What do you see as its advantages and disadvantages? What 'non-added-value' activities does it need to keep it functioning? Would any alternative models be beneficial?

What should we call 'HRD'?

Traditionally HRD reports to the wider HR function, although there are arguments to say it should have equal status or even belong to 'business development'. What is important is that the HRD director has access to the people and business information needed to carry out the role in the best possible way for the organisation.

Slowly 'human resources' is being replaced by 'human capital', a more 'asset-based' description – or by other titles such as 'people and culture' (eg Ericsson) or 'people and organisation' (Royal Mail). HRD needs to reflect the cultural approach to people management, and can choose from many options, such as:

- chief learning officer/learning consultants
- human resource development
- people development
- learning and development
- training and development

- intellectual capital development
- human asset development
- director, 'XX Learning Consultancy'
- director, 'XX University', 'XX Learning Academy', etc.

Titles have political implications, and affect the impression that people have of what someone contributes.

Roles and capabilities in the HRD community

There is scope for a number of roles, and no individual should expect to be skilled in all of them. The range needed will clearly depend on the *structural* choices made, and the mix of internal and external resources. We have emphasised the importance of capability frameworks for managing development effectively, and HRD should be a role model in their use.

Below we discuss the different roles involved in making people development successful. More than one role may be combined in one person.

First, *all employees and managers* should have an understanding of the learning process, of the learning cycle, of learning styles and methods, and what works for them. They should know how to use the people around them, how to share knowledge and access and utilise that of others. A knowledge of how to use technology tools to aid learning is essential today. Ideally, everyone should be skilled at giving and receiving constructive feedback.

The HRD director

The HRD director does need to have a very special profile. Not only should he or she be expert in their understanding of learning and in managing learning processes, but they also need to talk the language of their organisation's business fluently. That means an appreciation of the underlying 'technology' of their organisation, the issues involved in managing it, and the key roles and activities that are necessary. Above all, familiarity with the numbers that drive the organisation is key, and the ability to make cost and benefit calculations with credibility. Add to this the attributes of sociability, influencing, consultancy, listening, organisational sensitivity, risk-taking and functional leadership – add in a heavy dose of passionate pleasure in seeing people develop – and we have a scarce combination!

It will have been a considerable advantage to have worked 'in the line'; but my observation is that seconding to such a role line managers who do *not* have a passion for people development, or a real understanding of how people learn, is a disaster. If they cannot lead the function professionally they will rapidly lose respect.

Professional trainers

These are people who – either by virtue of their subject expertise, or for their interest in the training process – have made training their career. A range of specific competencies apply to them, including:

- how people learn
- training design
- materials design
- classroom delivery
- group facilitation
- using technology for learning
- individual coaching
- evaluation.

The CIPD in the UK provides a qualification in the form of a 'Certificate of Training Practice', and there are many other forms of specialised certificates that can be achieved. Trainers may be *internal* or *external*, and we look at the merits of choice on page 155.

Learning consultants

These are distinguished from deliverers as experts in the determination of learning objectives that will support business goals in the process of learning, and in the choice of learning needs and solutions. Their consultancy skills are central to them – coupled with strong background knowledge of the organisation and its goals, of the nature of the workplace and its pressures and demands, and of how people learn. They should be skilled in translating a problem (or opportunity) into learning needs, at any level in the organisation. They do not *start* with solutions and curricula. This is more than just being an expert in *learning* itself – it involves understanding the language, the pressures and the demands of the business. Many HRD people tend to believe the task takes care of itself, and problems need to be seen essentially in *people* terms. The effective consultant is knowledgeable enough to assess task, system and people components of a problem.

Managing consultants

In a consultancy-led HRD function, there is scope for a senior role to co-ordinate other consultants in a specialist area. Consultants may move around specialist teams depending on their own development plans. This role might also take on that of relationship manager, client manager or HRD business partner as needs and structure dictate. Such a person makes it his or her business to know intimately the operations and people of the business units for which they are responsible, combining personal credibility as a business-orientated learning expert with a passion for building a holistic learning culture.

Programme and project managers

HRD always has some ongoing programmes for which it is responsible. Here are some examples:

- graduate development
- high potential assessment
- high potential development
- general management development
- succession planning
- organisational change initiatives
- special skill change initiatives.

Particular skills here will include project and cost management, negotiation and communication. External people may assist with delivery, but ownership will always want to be with the HRD function itself.

Managing development programmes is not a 'paper' job – the person responsible needs to get out and meet as many of the people as possible that they are seeking to develop and understand their individual situation and context.

Project managers are needed also for change management programmes or other special initiatives, such as looking at the intellectual capital of a merger, joint venture or acquisition.

Developing people takes time. Continuity in directing programmes is fundamental to success, and particularly in management development an incumbency of at least three years is recommended.

Support staff

Essential contributors, these include event administrators, materials controllers, marketing staff and secretaries. The ratio of this group to the other categories is an important measure of efficiency, but if too low it can be seriously counterproductive. *Creative* people who can design learning materials and make them exciting and interesting in different media are also essential, although they may not be able to be resourced in-house

HR managers

If the HRD director sits centrally in an organisation, operational HR business partners, where they exist, may sometimes be seen as a barrier through their gatekeeping role. We look at the politics of this in Chapter 8, but ideally they should be seen as partners and a resource in their own right. Their role can include:

- agents of the HRD strategy

- champions of the desired learning culture

- a source of learning needs

- effective implementers of the HRD systems and processes

- deliverers of some learning solutions.

Senior management

It has been said that the overriding role of senior managers is to select good people and guide and coach them. In reality we know that some are excellent role models and some very poor. We may not be able to do too much to change the way they are, but we look to them to:

- be role models of the organisation's values, and of implementing people development processes

- support some learning and change programmes through attendance, presentation and listening/interaction

- give the right priority to funds and resources for people development

- be generous providers of learning opportunities

- communicate the right supporting messages

- contribute to the HRD strategy

- take a proactive interest in career management, enabling talented people to move across the organisation.

Line managers

It is often the case that the HRD specialists live in another world from line managers. After all, they think about learning issues all day, whereas for managers HRD issues may be low in their time allocation. (Despite exhortations to be more concerned about developing their people, the pressures put on most managers will ensure this situation does not change much.) However, they do have a unique and vital part in the learning and development of the people who work with and for them, since they decide who does what in the daily work. We have listed some of these.

The manager's role in a 'learning environment' is described well by Honey and Mumford (for details of questionnaires see the Peter Honey website, listed in References and Further Reading), looking at four parameters:

- being a role model of learning themselves
- being a conscious and generous provider of learning opportunities for others
- building learning into the daily systems of work
- being a champion for learning across the organisation.

Their questionnaire designed to self-assess these factors is helpful and enlightening – albeit I have often found when using it that managers respond, 'this is all very well and desirable, but where do we get the time to be so perfect?' This is a very real problem, and it is a task of the HRD director to be realistic and build into their expectations and processes what can be actually achieved by the majority of managers.

Line managers are resources in other ways. They may be *mentors* to others, particularly younger people such as graduates, assessors in development centres, resources in training exercises and givers of their own experience in learning events. Unless the organisation has a detailed time-based cross-charging system, they are a 'free' resource to HRD.

HRD should not make assumptions that all managers will fulfil all the roles that are desired of them. Those who are particularly interested and skilled in developing people should be used perhaps beyond their own team.

APPLICATION

Draw up a summary of the respective roles of HRD staff, HR, the line manager, and the individual in the people development arena today. Is there a case for any adjustment of these roles, and what would be the implications for capability for each of the contributors?

Mentors

A network of mentors throughout the organisation can be critical where emphasis is put on personal ownership of development. In some organisations mentoring is made available to all. HRD would be responsible for managing the network and mentor capability. Readers are recommended the specialist books on this area published by the CIPD.

A register of specialist expertise

As in all functions, individuals develop their own interests, and by virtue of their experiences develop *specialist expertise.* The knowledge of who has what should be made available for the benefit of all. In my time at ICL, we took some 100 specialist subjects, grouped under learning, organisation development, career management, performance management, skills and qualifications, resourcing and general. Each subject had a 'focus person' who took the lead in professional expertise (they may have been in HR or HRD anywhere in the world), and then up to five others could designate themselves as 'specially interested'. This 'register of expertise' was electronically available to all.

APPLICATION

Do you have an HRD capability framework? If not, what would be its basic structure? If so, how well does it meet the needs of the values, structure and roles that HRD needs?

Study some 'person specifications' for HRD staff in other organisations and see if there are some ideas to apply for yourself.

NETWORKS

Networks are an important resource both to the HRD director personally, and within the organisation. If the HRD director sees an accountability for knowledge transfer across the organisation, and recognises the need to 'create bridges across boundaries', they would work with business areas and functions to facilitate people coming together. The HRD director might well make a map of what is happening across the organisation – where are there flows of both person-to-person and electronic communication? Here is a checklist to be used for each department or division:

- What are the boundaries that potentially prevent people sharing together?
- In what ways and how often do they come together face to face?
- In what ways and how often do they communicate electronically?
- Who would be the catalysts for creating network activities?
- How can HRD help to facilitate them?

Perhaps the reader responds by saying, 'But this is not *my* problem!' The question, as discussed under knowledge management earlier, is: How accountable does the HRD director feel for organisational learning? If the ultimate accountability is to ensure it is maximised, the learning from others is a major contributor. So HRD may both initiate and manage networks itself – learning networks that follow up, as a group, a particular programme; common interest groups (such as people interested in self-managed learning) – the possibilities are endless, and – like Internet newsgroups – the goal is that they have a life of their own and need only occasional stimulation.

APPLICATION

How many networks is HRD involved in internally? What other opportunities can you see for initiating, facilitating or regenerating others?

The HRD director will want to learn from others too, and others external to the organisation. Good external networks and clubs are a key resource – for benchmarking, for finding out about good practice, for questioning one's approach and getting new ideas, and for 'plagiarising' from others. 'Networks of contacts' is included in our components of capability as distinctive and critical.

Some useful networks for HRD professionals are shown in Table 6.3, (as existing in 2004).

APPLICATION

How many networks do you and your colleagues belong to, internally and externally?

▷ Table 6.3 Useful networks for HRD directors

Association of Management Educators and Developers (AMED)	www.amed.org.uk
European Foundation of Management Development (efmd)	www.efmd.be
American Society of Training and Development (ASTD)	www.astd.org
European Human Resource Forum (ehrf)	ehrf@cix.co.uk
The Conference Board Europe	www.conference-board.org
Careers Research Forum	www.crforum.co.uk
Chartered Institute of Personnel and Development forums	www.cipd.co.uk
UKHRD Network	www.ukHRD.com
TrainingZONE	www.trainingzone.co.uk

EXTERNAL VS INTERNAL RESOURCES

Organisations today do not expect to find all their human capital from fully contracted employees, and training is one area where this is generally the case. There is a very wide range of suppliers available, specialised in particular fields, and no HRD department can expect to employ all the skills and knowledge needed.

A key question for the HRD director is, 'How do I decide the skills I should have in-house (if any)?' This is not so much a cost decision as one of *value*. Where do in-house staff have the capacity to add value over and above that which can be obtained externally? Here are some possibilities:

- They can have an in-depth understanding of the organisation, its people, its business and its strategies.

- They share in the common business goals and loyalties.

- They can build a network of contacts within and without the organisation.

- They enable the transfer of learning and best practice across the organisation.

- They can create centres of excellence that can be a competitive advantage.

A set of criteria can be drawn up to determine whether activities should be resourced in house on this basis of adding value.

Some pragmatism may affect the decision, such as 'headcount restrictions', the skill set that we already have, the volume of training required in a particular capability, and organisational policies on outsourcing. The development of human capital is a major strategic issue in building value, as argued in Chapter I, and the management of HRD overall, and of strategic programmes supporting the business, should never be outsourced.

APPLICATION

Do you have a clear description of where added value comes from in-house staff? How does your current portfolio stack up to it? Did you make compromises, and if so, why?

Learning partnerships

Apart from subcontracting one-off specific programmes and learning requirements, HRD may look for different forms of learning partnerships. These imply a longer term and broader relationship than a series of transactions.

Figure 6.2 Organisational Learning Partnerships

Figure 6.2 shows a map of different kinds of learning partnerships. There is much to be gained in partnerships with customers and suppliers – in mutual learning that will gain benefits for both sides. HRD may or may not be involved in facilitating these. Organisations also form relationships with individual gurus, either in their specialist fields or in business, and these act as ongoing advisers. Here we shall look specifically at educational establishments, business schools, and consultancies.

The use of consultancies

HRD may be subject to general organisational policies regarding the use of consultants; indeed, some exclude them on principle. Others have stringent guidelines for their use, including levels of spend, 'accreditation', references, contractual terms, or being on approved lists. The field of people development attracts a large number of consultants, ranging from the independent practitioner with his or her niche of expertise and client relations, to the large international firms. There is therefore plenty of choice. Long-term relationships enable consultants to share in the organisation development process and seriously absorb the culture. Areas of potential consultant help include:

- assistance with determining the strategic HRD framework – sometimes they can see an overview or collate views given to them from different sources, which adds a new perspective to that held by the HRD director

- working with top management to establish their considered approach to people development

- researching learning needs and client perceptions

- setting up learning partnerships

- designing, running and evaluating specific programmes

- designing and implementing systems and processes

- evaluation of resourcing choices

- programme/event evaluation and RoI calculations

- benchmarking with other organisations

- facilitating 'political' workshops or meetings

- presenting particular messages at corporate events

- talent benchmarking.

The choice of consultants is sometimes a nightmare for HRD due to the plethora of large, medium and individual resources available. Ex-staff are frequently used, or those where long-standing relationships exist. Trying out new resources is a risk, as there is rarely the opportunity for 'piloting'. Lists of clients in consultant's publicity may look impressive, but often go back years. It is therefore important to get focused references – not just on the company but on the individuals themselves with whom one might be working, and to be satisfied that they will provide the right 'chemistry' with the target audience.

Managing consultancies is a skill in itself, and worthy of study by HRD. The deliverables need to be very clearly agreed and investment in providing as much background as possible will pay off. Beware of those who want to bring standard solutions and look for evidence of good customisation. Fixed-price quotations, though helpful for budgeting, are not necessarily the best option as they will be loaded to cover contingencies. Agreed day rates and regular joint planning of the work to be done period by period may work out best for both parties. Some consultancies may look for payment as a proportion of value added by them. This is a good principle – but often in the HRD arena not easy to evaluate in financial terms to joint satisfaction.

APPLICATION

Study how consultants are being used in HRD activities across the organisation. Are there some consistent patterns? Taken as a whole, does it represent a sensible use of internal and external resources, given the talent available internally? Could there be other opportunities where consultants could add value?

Using business schools and other educational institutions

This is a significant area of collaboration, and many institutions promote the concept strongly as a source of continuing revenue and research. Some offers of 'partnership' are a way of securing an annual contribution with not too much in return other than an annual 'partners' dinner' and some preferential access to MBAs. But there are many advantages to organisations in a true learning partnership. Most of all is the potential to harness a business school's resources to seriously understand strategy and culture and to choose or develop learning materials that are highly relevant. Relationships with individual faculty members can extend into consultancy and coaching; internships can be offered; and a business school can become a partner in the management of change.

Business schools and other institutions offer a number of opportunities to assist with development, particularly of managers. These include a variety of MBA and Masters courses, varying in cost, quality, timing and content. These may be used by individuals (see pages 57–59), or an organisation may work with a business school on a customised version designed for their employees. If accreditation is sought, there are generally strict standards that have to be reached and a heavy academic input. Henry Mintzberg of McGill University Canada broke out of the MBA mould with his 'International Masters Programme in Practising Management', which lasts 18 months, takes place in four countries and focuses on 'the development of managers in their own contexts'. Participants who wish to receive the accredited Masters degree write an additional paper after the final module. This is a unique programme, unlike any other in its combination of depth and application.

Attending a major business school has considerable prestige, both for individuals and organisations. HRD needs to decide its policy on the use of available courses for *individual development.* Business school alumni are generally favourable to their alma mater and – if in a senior management position – may suggest to the HRD director that options are explored. Considerable clarity is needed as to the objectives of any programme – is it aimed to improve the general capability level of the executives as individuals (like many leadership development programmes), or is it seen as part of an organisation development programme? It may be both – but objectives should be clear. Many major organisational change initiatives benefit from shared learning and reflection by the whole executive or management team, built around the change and what it means. Business schools are expensive and HRD should ensure they are allocated a programme director who can really understand their needs and who cares about the programme's success.

What added value can a business school bring? It is rich in learning resources and can provide an ambience of innovation, exploration and discussion that may not be possible in other premises. It provides opportunities for networking that can have a special quality when combined with the ambience of the learning environment. Business schools today expect to offer virtual learning environments blended with classroom experiences, and have moved a long way from programmes consisting of a series of professorial lectures and well-worn case studies.

IN BRIEF

- Thorough needs analysis that is business driven will almost always yield more demand than can be met. A system of prioritisation is essential. We need to use systematic cost/benefit analysis but will always have to balance with political considerations. The model of comparing strategic impact with cost, population by population, will be helpful.

- We looked at different strategies for internal funding and pricing. The choice is strategic, as it will give potent messages to the organisation. If there are opportunities for external revenue generation, this should be a separate unit and not confused with looking after 'home'.

- Sometimes resourcing decisions are made *for* HRD, especially when it comes to premises and budgets. However, the more knowledgeable and prepared the HRD director is about the best use of resources, the better will be the ability to convince others of what he or she believes is right for the organisation. Never be caught by surprise budget cuts!

  When it comes to having a training centre, there are more considerations than cost. Would we benefit from a place that consolidates a desired culture?

  A vital strategy is the use of e-learning. HRD must keep a firm balance between cost attractiveness and effectiveness of learning.

- A vital decision for the HRD director is how to co-ordinate the different contributions to people development. This will lead to defining roles and a capability framework that will support it.

- Networking is a key activity for HRD – internally and externally. Not only should HRD have its own, but it is a part of its role to ensure a 'network of networks' exists across organisational boundaries.

- Choosing between internal and external resources should be driven primarily by the added value of internal staff, which should be utilised to the maximum. It is very easy to be diverted into activities that someone external could easily do.

■ HRD should explore the potential of different kinds of learning partnerships, as well as be able to use consultants effectively as a complement to internal resources.

■ REFERENCES AND FURTHER READING

CRAINER S. *and* DEARLOVE D. (1999) *Gravy Training: Inside the world's top business schools.* Jossey Bass.

KPMG CONSULTING (2001) *Earning through Learning: Global lessons in e-learning.* KPMG.

MEGGINSON D. (2003) *Continuous Professional Development.* London, CIPD.

MITCHELL, A. (1997) 'Defining the role of corporate learning centres and universities'. *efmd Forum,* Vol. 97, No. 3.

SLOMAN M. (2002) *The e-learning revolution.* London, CIPD.

SYRETT M. *and* LAMMINEN J. (1999) *Management Development.* Economist Books.

WELCH J. *with* BYRNE J.A. (2001) *Jack.* Headline Book Publishing.

www.beyondbudgeting.com

www.dell.com

www.elearningcentre.co.uk

www.impm.com

www.peterhoney.com

www.unipart.co.uk

7 ■ RETURN ON INVESTMENT

Sooner or later, HRD is going to be asked to justify its contribution, in whole or in part. As a business-oriented department, it should be able to respond to any request. However, this is easier said than done. Readers will know what a thorny and difficult path it is to good evaluation and to showing a return on investment.

In this chapter we look at the kind of measures that HRD should use to track its effectiveness and success, and briefly survey how project justification and return on investment is done.

It is not enough to qualitatively argue that 'the business is benefiting' from an activity. We need to be able to do the following:

- measure and monitor the efficiency of how HRD runs
- use time effectively
- measure the effectiveness of what HRD achieves as a department
- be able to justify a new programme or initiative
- be able to evaluate programmes at different levels
- benchmark with other organisations.

There are many excellent works covering this subject, and this chapter is but an overview of the factors to be taken into account in determining our strategy. A part of the strategy must be to make choices of what measures will be used, and when.

THE NEED TO BE NUMERATE

This is not always a feature of professionals working in people development. Their unique skills are the opposite to those of the accountant. However, someone in the department needs to be able to competently assess costs and understand the validity of measures and how they are used. In business, and even in most public sector organisations today, numbers speak louder than words.

One area of expertise is to know intimately how the accounting system works. One of the many failures of traditional accountancy is that it cannot distinguish between costs that contribute to value, and those that do not. The 'negative' expenditures of time, travel costs, equipment, etc are all lumped together with those that positively contribute to value for stakeholders. So many of the effects of the 'shadow side of organisations' are invisible to numbers-oriented management.

HRD will find it useful from time to time to make estimates of some of these hidden costs. Examples are the loss of productivity from poor leadership, the cost of duplication due to lack of knowledge sharing, the cost of resolving a customer problem that would not have happened if we had the right capability in place, or unwanted attrition due to poor management. We should be good at 'estimating', and answering questions like, 'What would be the effect of a 1 per cent productivity improvement?' HRD should be particularly aware of productivity measures in the different departments in the organisation – sensing opportunities for improvements.

THE EFFICIENCY OF HRD

Internally within HRD, as for all well-managed functions, there need to be standards of performance regarding administration, response times and quality – which should be assessed by internal monitoring and 'client' surveys (see next chapter).

The much-despised 'happy sheets' do measure a part of 'customer satisfaction'. Though they are not a good measure of learning that has taken place, they give valuable feedback in their own right regarding the acceptability of material, trainers, environment, and so on. It would be bad news if these were the only measure of success from HRD's efforts, however.

HRD will be interested in a number of factors in the training arena:

- ratio of support costs to delivery costs
- costs per trainee day
- trainer utilisation
- facilities utilisation (if relevant).

The distribution of competency levels in the function should be regularly compared with the ideal requirement.

Using time effectively

If we have set up HRD as a learning consultancy we may have a time recording system and know where time goes – but this is rare. This is a much-neglected area.

All departments are inevitably going to spend some of their time on 'internal maintenance', without any clear contribution to a stakeholder. A major aid in effectiveness is to have a clear understanding of what is and what is not 'added value' work. This is not what feels useful, but is what is directly related to adding value to stakeholders.

Accounting systems treat the work done by people as cost items such as 'wages and salaries', 'overtime', 'bonuses', 'benefits', 'pensions', 'social security', and so on. There is no distinction between the *proportion* of time spent that is actually adding any value to a stakeholder, and that which does not. An enormous amount of time may be consumed by such things as:

- car travel
- meetings about internal affairs
- reviews and updates
- reading superfluous e-mail
- managing problems that should not have occurred
- redoing work
- reports and information provision
- consultation for its own sake (ie it is unlikely to add value to the decision)
- internal negotiation and cross-charging
- arguing for resources
- mistakes, especially when repeated
- duplication
- waiting time
- computer downtime
- regulatory compliance.

Readers can add to this list from their own experience.

Even if not regularly recording time spent, the HRD director should ensure that from time to time samples are taken of a week's activities, recorded in two columns under the headings of 'value adding' and 'non value adding'. If the proportion of the latter is greater than one-third, some investigation should be conducted.

APPLICATION

Conduct a survey for a week on the way time is used in HRD. What is the percentage of non-value-adding work? Does it justify any action?

Adding value to a stakeholder in HRD would include all work *directly* concerned with growing our human capital – training, managing other learning programmes, deciding about career moves, coaching, and so on. It also includes work done aimed at increasing revenues and reducing costs, and any directly aimed at external customer satisfaction. HRD may also do things for the community as a stakeholder (young people secondment schemes, etc).

MEASURING THE EFFECTIVENESS OF WHAT HRD DELIVERS

Organisations sometimes describe their investment in learning as so many training days (or £ spent) per person per year. Like headcount, a crude and inaccurate measure of human capital, this is simple and the information reasonably available. It is not a measure of learning, which since it has so many facets is impossible to assess. But it is also only an *input* and not an outcome. A large part of those training days could produce nothing for the organisation by way of benefits. There are other inputs, such as the percentage of employees having development plans. But this does not tell us whether any development actually happened.

What kind of *output* measures would tell us that people development is actually occurring and that HRD's work adds some value?

Overall, we should be able to see that the sum of quantified benefits from the programmes that are run to improve capability substantially exceeds the *total* costs of HRD. A good target may be 'by at least 300 per cent'. As we see below, we cannot see the benefits of all we do in financial terms. Not all HRD work is aimed at immediate bottom-line returns. Nevertheless, where it can be calculated it should be done. One evaluates the full annual cost of the HRD function and its activities. Then, for those events that are aimed at a change in a business result, estimate any annualised cost savings, productivity changes or the value of new revenues resulting from the training. This is then summarised and compared with the annual costs of running HRD. Since many programmes will show a substantial return on their costs, this may not be as difficult as it sounds.

The extent to which learning goals are met is the best measure. This implies that they were sufficiently well articulated in advance as to be measurable afterwards. There will never be a problem with evaluation if the objectives are clear. They should always include one or more of the following:

- a defined increase in knowledge or skills
- achieving a qualification
- building a network
- experiencing some particular situations
- seeing a measured cultural change
- improving perceptions of employees or customers.

In career development and continuity management, we look for ratios that measure our success in the longer term, such as:

- percentage of positions with no successor coverage
- percentage of planned career moves that take place
- percentage of high potential people by function/division/area
- percentage of vacancies filled internally
- percentage of people with more than one year's international experience
- loss rate of high potential people and other high added value personnel, leaving due to perceived lack of career opportunity
- percentage of expatriates abroad for clear career development reasons
- percentage of people with the highest levels of our core competencies
- appropriate diversity statistics.

These can be divided up of course into relevant parts of the organisation, and this is recommended rather than averaging over the whole.

We have an interest in how key policies and processes are working, and should want to measure (for example):

- the percentage of people having appraisal and career discussions
- the percentage of *completion* of specified learning needs in personal development plans

- the percentage of people receiving professional or additional qualifications

- the percentage of people completing compliance training.

Finally, we want to assess how well we are actually supporting the strategies and drivers of the organisation. This would be a review with key people, collecting perceptions of 'clients', and making an honest judgement with a view to continuous improvement.

APPLICATION

What measures are you using today? Who takes an interest in them? How complete are they in relation to the above? Would you see benefit in introducing some new ones?

Costs and benefits – justifying and evaluating initiatives

There is no doubt that a lot of expenditure in HRD programmes is 'wasted' in the sense that the returns do not justify the cost. Informal estimation of whether a programme is valuable or not is more comfortable than the disciplines of systematic assessment.

Because this is not an easy area, HRD will rightly need to be selective about those initiatives that should qualify for the 'full treatment', but not use the fact that evaluation is a complex and time-consuming activity as an excuse for the wrong reason. Certainly, justification of major programmes and initiatives should be much more widespread and disciplined than it is.

Some criteria for the choice of projects worth evaluating might be:

- programmes over a certain level of expenditure

- pilots of a bigger programme (this is a generally excellent approach)

- highly visible and strategic programmes such as a major management development initiative, that may attract questions regarding their value

- projects involving significant external expenditure, such as outsourcing or consultant studies

- programmes that seek to help with a significant problem facing the organisation.

There are two types of RoI activity:

- preparing a case to justify a programme or project

- evaluating whether the programme or project met its expected returns.

The steps required in an RoI justification are:

1 Define the objectives of the programme.

2 Calculate the estimated costs of the programme.

3 Estimate the returns derived from the programme.

4 Balance the two and conclude that the programme is or is not a worthwhile use of resources.

If we want to evaluate and assess the impact of a programme, it requires considerable additional planning. There are many more steps – 11 are suggested below. Practitioners often start the process of evaluation after a programme or initiative has taken place. This is difficult to do because (a) the initial objectives may have been imprecise, and (b) the data we need have not been collected.

1 Define the objectives of the initiative.

2 Make a data collection and evaluation plan.

3 Collect data before the initiative if before/after comparisons need to be made.

4 Collect data during the initiative as needed.

5 Collect data after implementation.

6 Calculate all costs involved at each stage.

7 Isolate the effects of the programme from other factors that may have influenced the business impact.

8 Calculate the financial impact of the data.

9 Compare with the costs.

10 Present together with the non-financial benefits.

11 Judge whether the RoI was satisfactory.

Isolating the effects of training is a particularly tricky area and is what makes many evaluations difficult. Here are some factors to consider:

- Using control groups – one group receives training, the other does not, and comparing their respective performance.

- Trend lines can be used to predict the value of specific output variables if training is not undertaken. The variance is measured after training.

- A forecasting model can be used to predict the value of the desired output variable. Any shortfall or excess is attributed to the programme.

- Self-assessment – we can often identify the effect of our own learning.

- Line manager's assessment – through observation and effect.

- 360/450° assessment – subordinates, peers, line managers and customers, suppliers.

- Customer assessments – through improvements in efficiency, quality.

- Expert estimations – providers should have sufficient evidence to predict the likely output of a programme.

- Other influencing factors can be identified and factored out of the effect of the programme. The remainder is considered to be due to the programme.

LEVELS OF EVALUATION AND OBJECTIVE SETTING

In 1975 Donald Kirkpatrick developed four levels of evaluation for training. These are generally well known and were also described in broader HR terms by Jack Philips (see the website, listed in References and Further Reading) as:

Level 1 – general satisfaction by learners with their experience
Level 2 – learning achieved – measurable changes in capability
Level 3 – evidence of behaviour change
Level 4 – business impact.

Figure 7.1 shows a chain of value creation, which distinguishes between current benefits from learning and future benefits. Levels 1–3 will correspond to the lower boxes in the chain, but 'business impact' (Level 4) is more than the current financial bottom line. Many HRD activities are aimed at longer-term benefits – 'implementation of strategy', 'retention and commitment of stakeholders' and 'innovation'. They in turn will yield future financial benefits but it will be very difficult to calculate them related directly to a learning intervention. We need to see these categories as 'bottom lines' in themselves, and be able to measure change in them. Philips calls RoI evaluation Level 5, and suggests that, to be able to do this, measures at all the intermediate levels are needed.

In the box on page 170 is a test given to participants on a number of CIPD HRD strategy courses. No participant was able to complete it correctly – they showed a considerable lack of understanding of basic financial literacy. An answer is given on page 177.

For any programme or initiative, we have first to decide at what level it will be appropriate to evaluate, depending on the objectives of the activity. Some refer to the

Figure 7.1 Contributing to Value for Stakeholders

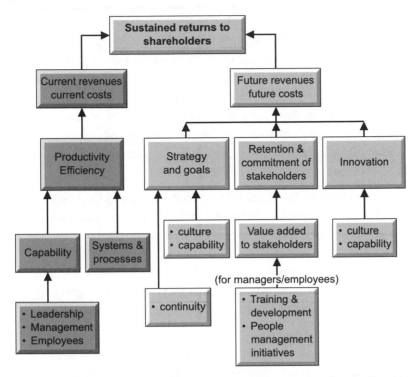

essential step of initial objective setting as Level Zero. It is so often done badly, without any clarity as to what will be achieved by the activity. It is the key to any evaluation exercise. Objectives can be set to cover increasing levels of measurement, aiming at a Level 4 indicator if at all possible.

Figure 7.2 shows a scorecard approach used for evaluating the impact of a major global management and leadership development programme.

Here are some examples of good objective setting:

> **❝** This training programme is aimed at increasing the level of participants in continuous improvement techniques to knowledge and skill levels 'C', with a view to improving the number of genuine cost saving suggestions to X per person per annum, to achieve annual cost savings of Y per cent per year in departmental operating costs. **❞**

> **❝** To develop leadership capability in order to:

■ provide a shared understanding of company strategy

TEST

150 high-potential middle managers from 40 different operating companies of a multinational telecommunications company were sent, in groups of 25, on a three-day management conference (MC). The MC consisted of group discussions to work out how the company values can be practically implemented, how change was taking place within the organisation to achieve the strategic business objectives, and also exercises to identify and share best practice. The direct cost per three-day programme (including travel and accommodation) was £60,000.

After attending the MC, it was noticed that the turnover for this highly mobile group dropped from 18 per cent to 8 per cent. Also, motivation levels of two-thirds of the group perceptively increased. This was supported by anecdotal and written evidence from appraisals (managers often reported gaining 'significant motivation' from the programme) and was also measured as an increase in productivity of the team being lead (generally this was found to be 10 per cent revenue or a decrease of 5 per cent costs per employee).

The average number of employees in a team is 10; the average materials and operating costs per employee are £70,000; the average sales per employee are £80,000. Fifty per cent of managers attending the MC have positions that are linked directly to revenues, and 50 per cent are linked to costs.

The average managerial salary (inc benefits and bonuses) is £100,000.

Evaluate the monetary value of financial (tangible) benefits, the monetary value of intangible benefits, and the return on investment.

■ achieve a 75 per cent level of confidence by staff in their leadership

■ increase financial added value/employee by 10 per cent in a two-year period. 〞

❝ To introduce a stress management programme for dept X in order to reduce stress-related absence by one third over the following 12 months and improve retention in this group by 25 per cent over the same period. 〞

All these examples have clear business benefit goals that can be measured. Sometimes programmes will be aimed solely at the demonstration of learning – a level of

Figure 7.2 A scorecard to track the impact of a major development programme

THE MEASUREMENT SCOREBOARD FOR THE EXECUTIVE BOARD														
Measure Unit	Opinion Survey /VOC Q	Q	Q	360° average A	B	C	Retention % experts	% talent	compet ave	Productivity M1	M2	M3	Potential and succession % in talent pool	% roles no succession	% key ext hires
Operations															
Partners															
e-Services															
Europe															
Japan															
Business Markets															
Service Providers															
Enterprise Markets															
Functional Support															
N.B. absolute figures should be accompanied by % change since last report															

knowledge or skill. Some indeed may be only at Level 1 – the goal was primarily motivational for the individuals or the team, and we want to know only that they enjoyed it.

There will be initiatives that are designed specifically to reduce costs. In this case some research will be needed to estimate the scale of the unnecessary cost.

Table 7.1 is an example of a research questionnaire aimed at a knowledge management initiative. This kind of analysis has several benefits:

- It unearths 'hidden costs' that do not stare out from any lines on the accounts.

- It brings an awareness of 'a problem to be solved'.

- It makes management aware of the 'cost of doing nothing' – which is always an alternative.

As Chris Galvin, ex-CEO of Motorola, is reported to have said when he set up the Motorola University:

❝ If you think the cost of learning is expensive, try the cost of ignorance. **❞**

▶ Table 7.1 Knowledge management study

■ Can you think of an occasion where you found someone else in the company was doing the same project as you? If yes, give a few details, including the approximate cost of the project.
■ Can you think of any sales project that was lost because we lacked enough information about the customer's needs or about what competitor's could offer? How much money was the deal?
■ Can you think of any situation that 'went wrong' and afterwards you discovered that (a) either the same mistake had been made before or (b) it was due to inadequate utilisation of existing knowledge? What did it cost?
■ How much time do you spend a month (approximate percentage) searching for information?
■ Do you have ideas for a better company or a new product/service that nobody seems to listen to?
■ Can you think of any external relationships that have been lost, and because of this we have lost sales opportunities? What was their (approximate) impact?
■ Can you think of any situations where you could not respond to a request through lack of skills available? What did you lose as a result?
■ The results of a sample of managers would be intelligently extrapolated to estimate the overall potential impact of a KM programme.

Calculating return on investment

The standard formula for Return on Investment is the following:

$$\text{Return on Investment} = \frac{\text{Benefits} - \text{Costs}}{\text{Costs}} \times 100$$

BENCHMARKING

Benchmarking with other organisations is a valuable exercise, and can be done on a number of fronts:

- How do we compare in terms of our beliefs and philosophies?

- How do we compare in terms of efficiency?

- How well do we link our activities into the business priorities?

- How do we compare in terms of achievement of key goals?

Table 7.2 shows some questions for use in checking HRD efficiency. Questions can look

▶ Table 7.2 Benchmarking against other organisations

1 What functions are included and not included in your HRD department?
2 What percentage of your training is managed centrally as opposed to within a local business unit?
3 What is the total absolute £ spend of running the *central* HRD function, and what is this as a percentage of corporate revenue and paycost? (exclude delegate salary costs)
4 What is the additional £ spend of locally run training events, both internally and externally sourced? As a percentage of local revenues and/or paycost?
5 What is the number of average off-the-job training days per person per year?
6 What percentage of (a) training design and (b) delivery is done (i) by internal staff and (ii) by external resources?
7 What is the ratio of support staff to delivery staff in your HRD department?
8 If you have central training premises, what is their cost per trainee day?
9 What is a typical per diem charge for a delegate day (a) with accommodation and (b) without accommodation?
10 What model do you follow for charging 'customers units' for the provision of central training?
11 Do you employ an evaluation policy? If so, what is it? What is the estimated Return on Investment for your HRD function?

at training and development for the whole population, or – preferably – break the population down into subgroups such as: senior management, middle/junior management, technical/professional, administrative and support, operational, young entrants, etc. Some other questions might cover:

- how budgeting and pricing is done
- levels of involvement in strategy
- methodologies for linking business goals to learning goals
- the value placed on training as a support for business change
- beliefs and principles
- needs analysis processes
- line manager involvement
- range of learning methods used
- use of accreditation and management education
- roles and skills in HRD and HR staff

- evaluation methods and results

- organisational learning and knowledge management.

All benchmarking should have clear focused objectives so that it does not result in masses of data that cannot lead to much action.

APPLICATION

Try these questions out for your own function. Are you happy that you are benchmarking enough and with the right questions?

IN BRIEF

- HRD does need to have numerate skills – not in everyone but certainly available to it. Not only do we need to talk the language of business but need to make good business decisions ourselves.

- We need to have a 'scorecard' to measure the efficiency of the department – its utilisation of costs and people, and the way time is used.

- Most importantly, we need to measure the effectiveness of what HRD delivers – in learning programmes, in process effectiveness, in continuity and career management, and in how well it is in fact supporting the business drivers.

- It makes no sense to try to prove that every programme directly influences bottom line measures. Too many factors are in play, and this may not have been the learning goal anyway. There are several valid 'bottom lines'.

- HRD should, however, be skilled at building cases for programmes and projects before they are started, and in evaluation methodologies. HRD needs a strategy – a set of guidelines – for when it will evaluate.

- Benchmarking against other similar HRD functions helps to keep our performance in perspective.

- Readers are referred to the sister volume in this series 'Evaluating Training' and to others specialist works.

■ REFERENCES AND FURTHER READING

BEATON L. *and* RICHARDS S. (1997) *Making Training Pay: A toolkit*. London, IPD.

BECKER B.E., HUSELID M.A. *and* ULRICH D. (2001) *The HR Scorecard: Linking People, Strategy, and Performance*. Boston, HBS Press.

BEDINGHAM K. (1999) 'The measurement of organisational culture' *Journal of Human Resource Management*, January.

BRAMLEY P. (1996) *Evaluating Training*. London, CIPD.

FITZ-ENZ J. (2000) *The ROI of Human Capital*. New York, Amacom.

FLAMHOLZ E.G. (1999) *Human Resource Accounting: Advances in concepts, methods and applications*. 3rd edn. Kluwer.

GRANOFF T. (2001) *A White Paper on the Procourse Method of Measuring Success*. ProCourse Scientific Advisory Board.

HESKETT J.L., SASSER W.E. Jr, *and* SCHLESINGER L.A. (1997) *The Service Profit Chain*. New York, Free Press.

HUSELID M. (1995) 'The impact of human resource management practices on turnover, productivity and corporate financial performance'. *Academy of Management Journal*. No. 38. pp635–672.

KAPLAN R.S. *and* NORTON D.P. (1996) *The Balanced Scorecard*. Boston, HBS Press.

KEARNS P. (2000) *Maximising the RoI from Training: Measure the value added by employee development*. FT/Prentice Hall.

KIRKPATRICK D.L. (1975) 'Techniques for evaluating training programs'. In *Evaluating Training Programs*. Alexandria, Va, American Society for Training and Development.

KIRKPATRICK D.L. (ed.) (1998) *Another Look at Evaluating Training Programmes*. Alexandria, Va, American Society of Training and Development.

MAYO A. (2001) *The Human Value of the Enterprise*. London, Nicholas Brealey.

MAYO A. (2004) *Return on Investment from HR*. Personnel Today Management Resources.

PHILLIPS J.J. (1997) *Return on Investment in Training and Performance Improvement Programs*. Houston, Tx, Gulf Publishing Company.

PHILLIPS J.J., STONE R.D. *and* PHILLIPS P.P. (2001) *The Human Resources Scorecard: Measuring the Return on investment.* Butterworth-Heinemann.

RUCCI A.J., KIRN S. *and* QUINN R.T. (1998) 'The Employee–Customer–Profit Chain at Sears'. *Harvard Business Review.* January–February.

www.e-validates.com

www.fissing.co.uk (HR benchmarking club)

www.franklincovey.com/jackphillips (website of Jack Philips Centre)

www.procourse.com (including 23-minute video presentation on Training Evaluation)

www.pwcservices.com (now embracing the Saratoga Institute)

ANSWER TO TEST ON PAGE 170

Monetary value of tangibles:

Turnover reduction = 15 managers $\times$ £100,000 = £1,500,000 (estimated cost of replacement, opportunity loss and retraining new hires = one year's salary).

Plus monetary value of intangibles:

Productivity and motivation of 50 per cent managers measured by sales = 50 managers x 10 in team $\times$ 10 per cent of £80,000 = 500 x £8000 = £4,000,000. Sales margin = 12 per cent so bottom-line benefit = £480,000.

Productivity and motivation of 50 per cent managers measured by costs = 50 managers $\times$ 10 in team $\times$ 5 per cent of £70,000 = 500 $\times$ £3500 = £1,750,000.

Total = £480,000 + £1,750,000 = £2,230,000.

Total programme benefits = £1,500,000 + £2,230,000 = £3,730,000.

Cost of programme: £360,000

$$\text{RoI }(\%) = \frac{\text{Programme Benefits} - \text{Programme Costs}}{\text{Programme Costs}} \times 100$$

= (£3,730,000 − £360,000)/£360,000 $\times$ 100

= 936 per cent.

8 ■ MARKETING AND POLITICAL CONSIDERATIONS

HRD is a supporting function, and inevitably takes second place to business operational priorities. To be proactive and influential requires competing for attention, and HRD needs political and influencing skills. It can, of course, just get on with its activities relatively undisturbed – until the next review of overheads starts to ask whether it is adding any value. It can be caught out if not regularly assessing its success on this and other parameters.

This chapter looks at a number of areas of achieving support for what we do.

▮ THE PLACE OF HRD IN MANAGERS' THINKING

Whereas much of what HRD does will be appreciated, the truth is that developing people is not at the top of any manager's in-tray. I had a salutary lesson in my own career. As a result of restructuring, my job as HR manager was halved and I was offered a software marketing role. This was a great challenge and probably the most developing job I ever had, in particular teaching me more about politics in a short time than I could ever have learnt in HR. What surprised me was how rapidly I lost interest in anything to do with HR and in any other part of the organisation except my own, exciting and absorbing business objectives. When I returned to HR I had a different perspective of managerial priorities.

All organisations have their political 'maps', rather like 'snakes and ladders' boards. Altruistic employees who deplore politics in organisations are merely ignorant of the ways in which people work together – people with potentially competing objectives, overlapping accountabilities, individual power and influence aspirations, and genuine passions about the way things should be done. Politics can be divided into the 'natural' – defined by Rosemary Harrison (2001) as *the art of achieving the possible* – and into 'powerplay' where the aims of an individual or group may not be synchronised with the goals of the organisation. It is often believed by, for example, business school professors, that organisations continuously *seek* rational models for their decisions and behaviours. They may well value these, but other factors muddy their actions and decisions. *Homo organisationalis* is complex and all too human.

We have to remind ourselves of course that HRD has no given right to exist as a function except in so far as it does add value to the organisation. As we have seen in this book, this should not be difficult. But just as HRD sits in a political sea, it may well have an agenda of its own, for example:

- survival

- growth

- higher status

- influencing acceptance of its own values or interests

- new or different facilities

- wanting or not wanting to be outsourced

- external revenue generation

- public recognition through external conferences and publications.

This book is focused on how to do the right things for the *organisation* and we shall proceed on the basis that the HRD director has the greater interests of the organisation at heart and look at some of the issues that influence their effectiveness.

PRODUCING THE STRATEGY

Following the paths suggested in this book will involve a lot of conversations with both strategic and operational people. Some will not start from nothing; others with a clean sheet. We may find ourselves asking questions that are not expected from 'trainers', appearing to challenge business goals through probing questions. When going down this route for the first time, some explanation of *why* we are doing it will be necessary, always emphasising that our goal is to help *them* be more successful.

In many cases HRD is an integrated part of a broader HR function, and the senior HR director is the key player. HRD needs to seek empowerment to have the right discussions at the right level itself, and may need to negotiate some politics and barriers within HR as a prelude.

To produce an entire strategy from scratch may take some time, and may best be done in phases – phases that can be checked out with appropriate people as we go along. It will be surprising if the exercise does not result in proposing *change* – to policies, processes or to established programmes. The understanding of the need for change may be a mini-project in itself, talking with the stakeholders in the change and getting them on board.

ENGAGING EMPLOYEES IN THEIR OWN DEVELOPMENT

We have emphasised the benefits of all employees being able to manage their own learning. But why should they? (ie 'What's in it for me?' – WIIFM) Many employees associate learning with failure – a basis of the foundation of Rover's Learning Business.

The WIIFM for employees varies. Those who have ambition and/or curiosity have no problem with motivation. Some will come to courses willingly – not for the learning but for a break from routine. If 'learning to learn' workshops are routinely offered, then part of them should be exploring the potential benefits. They include:

- fun – learning can be fun and should be enjoyable

- competence – being more confident in their ability to do the job

- personal growth

- preparation for promotion; more money and status

- achievement

- security – preparation for potential job change that could be forced on all of us.

If the learner has no motivation it is very likely that the learning cycle will not be completed. So achieving that motivation is a major challenge for HRD professionals and managers, and worthy of a 'strategy' of its own.

A SHADOW SIDE TO ORGANISATIONS

Uncomfortable as it is for many, there is always a 'shadow' side to organisations, despite all the grand visions and values and promises that are written down and published, or formally discussed in meetings. Late night bar discussions usually surface it all! In daily life, this substantially influences productivity, stress levels, motivation and commitment, and the quality of life.

Politics in organisations is about steering through this shadow side, and includ obstacles such as:

- *organisational walls*. Structures create boundaries, which condition the behaviour of people. Even if previously co-operating, departments can start competing as shared objectives give way to rival ones. Communication becomes constrained across the boundaries, and people focus inwards within their organisational space.

- *business and organisational gaps*. These are like white space on an organisation chart, where accountabilities are owned by no one and it is impossible to grasp a lever for change.

- *idiosyncrasies and personal agendas of individuals*. Inevitably people use organisations to satisfy their own drivers and ambitions, and these may not be at all synergistic with the organisation's strategies. (Some organisational cultures are more powerful than *any* individual, but they are rare.)

- *national and local cultures and traditions*. The way things are done 'here' is, and always will be, different.

The effect of any of these may be to work against the logical systematic approach we have taken in following our model.

TOP MANAGEMENT SUPPORT

In order to be aligned with the business at all, some level of top management support and interest is essential. It is usually the case that the CEO, or equivalent, sets patterns that others follow, and his or her priorities and values are closely observed.

Table 8.1 shows some of the characteristics of different levels of support. To some extent this is a hierarchy of desirability. The chief executive who has a personal conviction of the vital support HRD can give to the organisation is of course a great asset, even if he or she makes life uncomfortable for the HRD director. If it is shared only superficially by other senior players it can be dangerous, as a widespread base of support is needed. Co-operation because it is 'politically correct' to do so may be only half hearted. So the second level in the table is highly desirable, and gives the HRD director regular access to dialogue with the team as well as endorsement of priorities.

Specific sponsorship for sections of HRD activity is also valuable for maintaining close business links. Thus the marketing director may sponsor all programmes connected with the development of sales and marketing people. It is often the case that cultural change, or for example, leadership initiatives, will be sponsored by the HR director. There are advantages in an operational director driving them, however.

Table 8.1 Levels of management support

Type of support	Characteristics	HRD response
CEO drives HRD agenda personally	HRD involved in major strategic decisions Priorities set by CEO Constant review by CEO	Close contact with business issues Flexibility of resources Strong influencing skills
Top team full commitment	Regular briefings/dialogues take place Priorities debated and agreed Focus on return	Use top team commitment as backer of messages Involve directors in appropriate programmes
Individual director sponsorship	Driving force behind sponsored programmes	Exploit business advantages of sponsorship and seek to extend
Subcommittee of board as 'steering group'	Likely that HRD director is secretary Reviews programmes and suggests advice on priorities	'Manage' the committee Use decisions effectively
'Passive' CEO support	Signs documents relating to HRD on request Shows support when asked	Utilise willingness to give desired messages Seek greater interest
HR director as champion	HR represents views of HRD and board	Thorough briefing Close familiarity with HRD
No representation	Control by budgets	Seek better representation

One useful approach is to have a 'people development steering committee', chaired by a senior executive committee member who is a good champion of HRD, and including other line managers. This provides a platform not only for guidance but also for exploration of ideas, sharing of thoughts on priorities, and feedback from the line. Such a committee can play a very helpful role in reviewing and contributing to the HRD strategy.

APPLICATION

Which levels of support do you enjoy at the moment? Which would you like to have? Do other support functions have more interest taken in them? If so, analyse the support they have and see why it is. Are there some lessons to be learnt?

Talk to some HRD directors in other companies and assess their level of support. Is there anything to learn from how they have achieved what they have?

Put together a plan for increasing the level of support from senior management.

CHALLENGING TOP MANAGEMENT

Top management not only decides the direction of an organisation, but may also prescribe the routes to achievement in some detail. Their view of change and of people development is frequently coloured by their own personal values and motivations, and more often than not dominated by 'bottom-line' considerations. They sometimes need to be guided into the perspectives of people lower down. The tendency to go for the 'blanket' solution is an easy way to show action to shareholders, parent companies or employees. A classic case is the response to poor customer satisfaction results – where the knee-jerk reaction may be to put everyone through a 'customer care programme'. It may well be the case that the front-line people are the last who need this – the *cause* of the dissatisfaction lies in lack of resources, inefficient logistics, a lack of management visibility or a host of other reasons.

Copying what other organisations do is also prevalent, and this may be encouraged through consultants and CEO clubs, who give senior managers ideas. The HRD director needs to have a firm grasp of what makes learning effective and really challenge where needed.

HRD needs to be skilled in deploying different influencing modes. It will be on safe ground if it can argue on firm business principles, and understand well at the same time what matters most to the senior manager. The HRD director should ask, 'What do I believe this person wakes up worrying about on Monday morning?'

ANALYSING THE LEVEL OF INVOLVEMENT IN STRATEGIC DECISION AREAS

In Chapter 1 we outlined some areas of involvement with business strategy. There are three levels of involvement that HRD can have in the business drivers that we have described in Chapters 2 and 3. They are as follows:

- *Defining* – part of the group that decides on the outcome

- *Consulting* – providing specialist advice to, or perhaps facilitating, the group in its decision-making

- *Implementing* – making the decision a reality.

We should not expect HRD to be 'defining' all these, whereas we do expect them to be supporting the implementation of all using learning. Each HRD director needs to decide the extent to which, if 'backwards integrated', they believe it would be helpful for the organisation and HRD. Extensive involvement for its *own* sake may increase the standing of the HRD director but may be very time consuming.

Table 8.2 can be used to quickly check out the level of involvement we have, and areas we should like to penetrate further. The last column refers to the ways in which involvement takes place. This might include some or all of the following:

- membership of strategic planning committees

- membership of performance improvement teams

- membership of quality circles

- membership of change management teams

- membership of new product introduction teams

- attendance at operational business reviews

- facilitating strategic workshops for business teams

- 1:1 dialogues with managers

- focus groups with cross-boundary groups

- systematic training needs analysis

- leading or belonging to task forces and special project teams

- performance appraisal consultancy.

▷ Table 8.2 Strategic partnership – levels of involvement

Business link	Involved in defining	Consulting to line management	Implementing through learning	Examples of involvement
Mission/vision/ strategic goals				
Values				
Beliefs in people development				
Defining core capabilities				
OD strategy				
External trends				
Business strategies				
Business goals and plans				
Change programmes				
Organisational change plans				
Human resource plans				
External/environmental changes				
Individual manager/team goals				
Operational problems				
Team and individual learning needs				

APPLICATION

Do the exercise in Table 8.2 for the part of the organisation for which you are responsible. Do not overstress the 'defining' elements – choose where you really feel HRD's involvement would make a difference.

Who might be able to help you close some of the gaps?

GAINING SUPPORT AND INFLUENCE

As in all relationships, finding a *bridge* to what someone cares about or believes in is what gives us an entry point to them. How can the HRD director change perceptions and exert influence?

- by finding out what interests and preoccupies a 'target' – an executive or a business unit – showing interest in what they do and a prime concern for supporting their objectives and agendas

- by demonstrating an understanding of the business or operations; what the key measures are, and what challenges/problems are being experienced

- by making formal connections into business decisions through membership of project teams, review bodies and steering groups

- by demonstrating real bottom line and organisational effectiveness gains from well-managed training interventions

- by achieving some 'quick wins' that have high visibility, and are both useful and exciting, gaining interest from others who were not involved

- by publicising success stories internally, especially those that affect business results

- by gaining good publicity for the organisation through the media and public platforms

- by creating strong links with people who influence the organisation as a whole and creating added value for them

- by sound benchmarking with competitors or leading organisations and questioning the positioning of one's own organisation against them (a good question for top management is: 'If competitors are investing more than we are in developing their people, what implications does this have?').

The location of the HRD function can make a big difference. How close is it to the

▷ Table 8.3 The balance sheet of credibility

Assets	Liabilities
Business knowledge and experience	No experience other than HR or HRD
Business understanding	Expert knowledge in guru-speak
Listening to business problems with interest	Talking psycho-babble and seeing every problem as having a soft-centred solution
Logical argument	Emotional argument
Accepting reality	Refusing to accept the shadow side of organisations
Working with reality	Working with dreams and idealism, living in hope of utopia
Respect for all	Respect only for perceived role models
Personal charisma	Skewed personality
Cares passionately about people development, rejoices in their success	HRD is just a job to be done
Self-aware; conscious of other's perceptions	Unaware of impact of own behaviour
Social skills	Unwilling to socialise
Persuasive skills	Dogmatic style
Problem-centred consultancy	Solution-centred prescription
Helps people learn from each other	Wants to control learning
Natural sharer and collaborator	Internally focused, jealous of personal knowledge
Takes time to network, internally/externally	Lost in a personal world
Understands the need for short-term gains	Expects people to buy into the long term
Looks for opportunities to help and support	Looks for opportunities to push own agenda
Looks for allies and works with them	Comes in tangentially
Able to manage the 'shadow side'	Regards politics as irrelevant
Money conscious	Regards money as a nuisance factor
Data oriented	Deals in immeasurables
Takes time to get to know people personally	Works through paper and e-mail
Brave in standing up for values and beliefs	Blows with the wind
Does what he/she promises	Enjoys talking rather than doing
Talks about success in managers' language	Talks about success in HRD language
Flexibility and adaptability	Looks for perfection

people with power? Is it siphoned away in the corporate university, giving the image of being in an 'ivory tower'? Or does the HRD director bump into key people frequently, sit with them in the restaurant, and keep close to what is happening in the business?

The personal credibility of the HRD director

This will be a powerful door to opportunities and influence. It is not just a question of being viewed positively by colleagues in the various parts of the organisation – unfortunately there are also risks of 'negative credibility', and image is a notoriously fickle creature.

Table 8.3 is a suggested 'balance sheet' of *personal* credibility. (It inevitably reflects the author's personal experience, and that is limited to the organisations he has worked with and the lessons he has had to learn himself.) This is a somewhat unstructured 'capability' profile of an HRD director. Not all items have the same weight, and much depends on the political and cultural environment as to what would be regarded as desirable.

APPLICATION

Ask some line managers what they would add, modify or delete in Table 8.3. Then ask some people you feel important to influence how they would score you from 1 to 10 on each line. (This could be done on an anonymous 360° format if desired.)

What lessons for your own development can be concluded?

Maturity in a support function is learning to work with and from reality, rather than wishing it was not there.

TESTING PERCEPTIONS

A study conducted by Ian Rose (1995), a Canadian researcher, found from looking into a large number of major corporations that the principal measure used to gauge the value of training is management's perception of the training department and its services. Some of the things that are looked for are detailed in Table 8.4.

We should regularly sample our 'customers' – all of the contributors to the HRD wheel – as to their perception of the added value of what we do. As the department of

▷ Table 8.4 Measuring management's perception of the HRD department

Business focus

- It has a thorough understanding of the business, listening to where the business wants to go, and determining what needs to be in place on the human side.
- It works forwards from the strategy of the organisation rather than backwards from the department's own agenda.
- It sees training as a lever of change and puts a lot of effort into 'organisational learning'.
- It is seen by the business as a prime resource providing essential services.
- It is always looking ahead to ensure the people are prepared for what is coming down the road.

Culture change

- It plays a key role in supporting, and at times even shaping, the culture of the organization.
- It provides a common core curriculum for mission-critical skills, including active and continued support for vision and values.

Customer focus

- It develops training strategies in partnership with customers.
- It has regular contact with customers and a thorough understanding of their business needs, and how to tailor internal training to meet them.

Focus on performance

- It sees its mission as way beyond the design and delivery of training interventions, but rather to help organisational units and individuals achieve performance improvement goals through provision of effective learning opportunities.
- It is an integrator with other functions within and beyond HR.
- It invests resources in the understanding of effective learning at all levels.
- It acts on a consulting basis to help reduce the need for training by encouraging (and helping with) alternative learning methods.

learning, preaching the importance of feedback as a learning tool, HRD needs to role model this and other learning principles. Table 8.4 provides a good basis for a diagnostic questionnaire. 'Happy sheets' from events are not a substitute.

Figure 8.1   Hertfordshire County Council's development charter

A MESSAGE FROM THE CHIEF EXECUTIVE

This Development Charter is intended to give a very clear message about the high level of commitment we have to your personal development and the commitment we want you to have to your own learning.

It is only by developing our staff and equipping them with the skills and knowledge they need, that we will be able to meet the challenges of the agenda the Council has set itself to take us into the next millennium.

It is our aim to create a culture of learning and, to ensure that we make progress we are setting ourselves performance indicators and targets for training and development which will be monitored by both Chief Officers and County Councillors. We will also be evaluating the Development Charter and its impact and I look forward to hearing about the changes that you have been able to make.

Bill Ogley
Chief Executive

DEVELOPMENT CHARTER

As an employee of the County Council I will be working in an organisation in which learning is valued. I will be supported to undertake the training and development which I need to help me to achieve and maintain a high standard of performance and will be given the encouragement and support to achieve my full potential.

I am entitled to:
- equality of opportunity in all aspects of my development
- an induction programme into my own job and department as well as the wider organisation
- an understanding of the direction and objectives of the Council and of my department
- an understanding of the contribution which is expected from me
- clear and measurable objectives for my performance at work
- an annual review of my performance
- a personal development plan which addresses my development needs. This will include on and off job development as well as personal learning
- a manager who is committed to staff development

I will be encouraged to undertake:
- continuous learning and development throughout my employment
- development to enhance my career prospects
- day release training to obtain the qualifications which I need to do my job
- planned work experience in a different department or organisation to broaden my skills and knowledge
- a planned and self-financing sabbatical where appropriate

I recognise that learning is a personal responsibility and I will therefore:
- share responsibility for identifying my development needs
- take advantage of development opportunities
- take an active part in performance management and staff development schemes
- take the initiative when I recognise opportunities for learning
- share my knowledge with others

MARKETING AND PUBLICITY

Publicising statements of principles

As we outlined in Chapter 2, it is immensely helpful to an HRD director to have an agreed 'charter' as a guide for their activity. If such does not exist, then should the HRD director just do his or her best, or actually seek such a statement? Many would compose one themselves and submit it to top management for their approval (and probably get it). It will be more powerful, however, if top management can define it in their own words and preferably jointly as a team. Several solidly business-based reasons can be given for asking a top team to do this – not least to guide the HRD director to spend their resources 'strategically'.

We gave at the end of Chapter 1 a number of examples of corporate statements of one kind or another, many of which declared beliefs in some way. An example of a freestanding statement is that of Hertfordshire County Council, called their 'Development Charter' (see Figure 8.1).

Often the beliefs behind people development are visible to employees through the processes that support it, and the documentation they receive. Thus, British Telecom launched a 'Partnership' in career development and had a series of interlinked strands with their accompanying booklets explaining them. ICL produced three booklets in a series 'Investing in People' – covering performance management, managing learning, and managing careers – which made clear the company's beliefs and the involvement of individuals in the three areas.

APPLICATION

List all the various documents available to managers and employees in your organisation that relate to people development. Note all the statements they contain that are 'beliefs' or 'values' related to development. Are you happy with what you have, or could you envisage a more coherent statement of beliefs that would be helpful to all?

Marketing HRD as a whole

Internal marketing sometimes seems to absorb more creativity and effort than that which is focused on real customers. Nevertheless, it has to be done, and it follows the same rules as any other kind of marketing. It is to do with image and reputation (perceptions), and with clarity of communication as to its purpose and ability to help. It requires:

- a memorable and sensitive 'branding', that gives the right message yet is sensitive to any potential negative reactions (ICL Learning gave itself the strapline 'Systems Integrators in Learning', which reflected the business strapline of the time)

- the 'liftspeech', which describes succinctly what HRD's role is

- using language that people easily relate to (avoiding HR jargon)

- understanding who potential 'customers' are, and clearly communicating messages to them that strike chords for them

- developing continuing relationships with key influencers

- making it easy for 'customers' to find out how HRD helps and what it offers (quality documentation, webpages)

- making it easy for 'customers' to do business with HRD (helpdesks, e-mail, html links)

- monitoring feedback and satisfaction with events and services regularly

- responding to complaints and difficulties promptly.

History is always with us. Training may have had low status, populated by ex-operational managers deemed to have failed at their jobs or been 'put out to grass'. They may have established themselves as course providers, and not be seen to have any strategic impact at all. Organisationally, they may be seen as tucked away in a cul-de-sac. So credibility may have to be built through a steady plan of discussion and publicity. The HRD director would look for opportunities to:

- present to the top management committee

- present to business unit team meetings

- take part in corporate conferences

- involve senior managers with business schools

- exploit intranets, webpages and other corporate communication media

- feature HRD staff and their achievements

- go in for any departmental competitions, corporate prizes, etc.

APPLICATION

What methods of communication and publicity are you using today? How are they perceived by the people you are trying to help (ask a few informally)? What could you do more effectively, or could add to your current range?

One part of a learning partnership may be to offer expertise and help in HRD to real customers of the business. Without necessarily selling any services to them, a seminar or discussion group can be set up that shares HRD's thinking and programmes. Business managers will appreciate this support and talk about it to others if done well.

Another is to offer a prize, for example for 'excellence in learning initiatives'. People can be nominated, a jury set up, and winners announced with suitable fanfares. Not only can good learning ideas be promoted, but also the role of HRD in encouraging learning *wherever it happens.*

Telling people what we plan to do

We may well have put together a strategy, with key directions and prioritised activities, that is absolutely business driven and designed in every way to support business achievement. That does not mean that everyone will automatically play his or her part.

Once again, we need influencing skills and the secret, as always, is to understand the needs and values of the person/people we are talking to. Logic and business need are not enough, important as they are. One may well get acceptance of an idea, but no real support because there is no answer to the famous WIIFM question – 'What's in it for me?' The greater good of the organisation as a whole, or longer-term benefits, may strike no chords in someone expecting to move on in a couple of years, or for whom current local success is absolutely predominant in their thinking. So we have a spectrum of 'partnership' by key players in our strategy (see Figure 8.2). Achieving the left-hand end of the scale is not difficult. After all, HRD deals in 'making things better, improving

Figure 8.2 A spectrum of partnership strength

Passive acceptance	Agreed support	Total commitment
'seems like a good idea'	'count on me to play my part when necessary'	'please get me and my people actively involved'

performance, developing people' – few will dispute the desirability of the offerings. But engaging hearts as well as brains, and then feet and hands, is a sales process. Selling is about helping people to clarify *their* need, and then showing how that need could be met. This is the essence of the learning consultant's core skill.

APPLICATION

Create a 'map' of support in the organisation – take top managers, other HR professionals, key line managers and other support functions. Use as axes 'strategic importance for HRD' and 'strength of support'. What factors contribute to the different positionings? How could you strengthen support where needed?

When it comes to *information*, we need to follow all the rules of marketing – helping the right people to know the right things at the right time. This may need a series of communications covering different groups of people.

Telling the organisation the good things we have done

Successful programme delivery is our best publicity. Making the strategy happen gives HRD a real chance to demonstrate their ability to contribute to business and personal success.

Business is no different to life – we like to back winners. Demonstrating the success of a strategy and its resultant initiatives is critical for preparing the ground for future strategies. Perhaps the initial strategy in a particular year was scaled down or not given the budget it required for implementation. Demonstrating success allows a second opportunity at a later date to revisit old ideas, or to introduce more daring ideas, or simply to gain support for the department.

Wherever we can show that an initiative has made a measurable difference to an important business measure, we should spread the news; likewise, we should celebrate individual achievement.

Publicising success stories is a powerful form of marketing. Again, internal media can be used – but also external. Speaking at conferences and seminars; writing articles (eg for *People Management*, *The Training Journal*, *Organisation and People*) and contributing to website interchanges gives publicity both internally and externally, especially if the company runs a 'cuttings service' for senior managers.

Some care and political judgement is needed nervertheless. We want to avoid attracting criticism from one section of employees for what they might see as preferential treatment for others. And an all too common occurrence is for the conference speaker from HQ extolling her or his company's latest initiatives, only to find a colleague in the audience who has never heard of them.

Going for awards

Organisational life today abounds with awards and the ceremonies and publicity that go with them. In the UK the best known are the National Training Awards (www.nationaltrainingawards.com) awarded both regionally and nationally, but various publications run 'Excellence Awards' with categories for learning and development or career management. The decision to make the effort to apply for one of these awards needs to balance the motivating effect for the professionals involved with the business benefits. Time and cost will be involved, and the main benefit is likely to be in an enhanced employer image, both internally and externally.

To achieve the government's 'Investors in People' award (www.iipuk.co.uk) is more about achievement of a set of standards, and has additional different benefits, albeit more pain in gaining the achievement. It may well be a useful influencing strategy in encouraging management to embed the sound people development practices that are required for the award. These practices themselves are likely to benefit the organisation in the more focused application of learning spend. Since its introduction in 1993, the award has helped many organisations, especially SMEs, to move towards a more strategic approach to learning and development.

APPLICATION

What does HRD's 'cuttings book' look like for the past two years? List any opportunities for telling the world good things you have done.

CONFLICTING MESSAGES BETWEEN HR AND HRD

Regardless of reporting relationships, it is often the case that HR and HRD are very busy in their own right pursuing their separate goals, and may not be well co-ordinated.

▷ Table 8.5 Possible differences between HR and HRD messages

HRD approach	HR approach
Career development is about continuous personal growth	Progress is visibly through going up the grading system
Personal ownership of careers and development is ideal	Job descriptions emphasise managerial control of development
We need people with a flexible and adaptable mindset	We must have consistency of terms conditions and benefits
We must reward people for the value they bring to the organisation	We must pay people according to the value of their job
We should see job vacancies as learning opportunities	We should fill each job with the best candidate available
The appraisal system is primarily about development	The appraisal system is primarily about performance management
We should always try to retain people who are valuable assets	We cannot afford what is not in the headcount plan

HRD is frequently associated in managers' minds with HR, and this can be a problem to either side, depending on their respective credibility. The greatest danger is that of mixed messages.

Table 8.5 gives some examples of where confusion may arise. One side represents a view of organisations as concerned with maximising and valuing *individual growth;* the other one is about hierarchical systems of consistency and control into which individuals are fitted. Hopefully, these dichotomies do not exist, but it is quite likely that the two sides are moving at different paces. Individuals may embrace the mindset of the left, only to find that the right is not yet ready to reinforce it.

Although it could be said to be firmly in the court of the HR director to avoid these confusions, the HRD manager will want to assist in the co-ordination of messages.

FINAL THOUGHT

We have observed before that, because many HR and HRD practitioners think that what they are doing is leading-edge practice, *and* they can show a logical link to business benefit, key business managers should welcome their efforts with open arms.

In my first HR role reporting to a managing director, Tony, I followed the due process of the time and asked him to set my objectives for the year. He thought for a minute and then said:

> **"** Andrew, I wouldn't have selected you if I felt you could not determine what needed to be done professionally yourself. I will judge you on the basis of whether your colleagues on the management team find you helpful in the achievement of *their* business goals. **"**

I was often conscious of the desire to do so-called 'leading-edge' projects, and – it must be said – gave in to that desire from time to time, but Tony's simple message is one I never forgot.

IN BRIEF

- HRD cannot escape from being in the political arena. To be strategic means being involved in all parts and at all levels of the organisation. It has to learn how to cope with 'the shadow side' of organisations and when it is appropriate to influence and seek change.

- It needs to evaluate where its support resides, and who are its champions. It may need to create some more of these and extend its reach of support; this can be done by many means, all involving effort and dialogue.

- In addition, HRD should evaluate its actual and desirable involvement in the strategic drivers and assess whether this should be extended.

- Credibility of any support function is the key to influence. HRD needs feedback as to how it is perceived, as does the HRD director personally, and this should be actively sought.

- Internal marketing is essential – of the function and its role, of its activities, and of its successes. Good publicity is powerful marketing in its own right.

- Setting up HRD steering groups of respected people in the organisation can be a powerful source of influence as well as guidance.

- We need to beware of conflicts in approach and message between HR and HRD, and do our best to ensure they are resolved.

- At the end of the day, will managers say we *helped* them – as individuals, yes, – but also in their business achievements?

REFERENCES AND FURTHER READING

GILLEN T. (1999) *Agreed! Improve your powers of influence.* London, IPD.

HARRISON R. (2001) *Learning and Development.* London, CIPD.

ROSE I (1995) *Measuring the Value of Training.* Research report. Vancouver, IBR Consulting Services.

ULRICH D. (1997) *Human Resource Champions.* HBS Press.

APPENDIX A: CREATING A LEARNING AND DEVELOPMENT STRATEGY

DRAFT STRATEGY TEMPLATE

1 Purpose(s) and audiences(s) for this HRD strategy (pp21–23)

2 Principles and beliefs about people development in our organisation (if explicit, give references) (pp40–49):

3 Mission and vision of HRD (pp84–85)

4 The populations to be considered in this strategy (p54)

5 The key 'drivers' to be supported:

   (a) vision, mission and values (pp32–38)

   (b) long-term strategic goals (pp34–37, 70–72)

   (c) strategic and core competences (p52)

(d) OD strategy (p53)

(e) external factors (p53)

6 Programmes that will support the above with their objectives (pp63–64)

7 Specific initiatives to support current business goals and change initiatives, with their objectives (pp73–76)

8 Specific initiatives aimed at remedying performance problems, with their objectives (pp77–80)

9 HRD-related policies (pp55–62)   *have*   *need*

10 Processes and tools (pp62, 63)   *have*   *need*

11 Implementing this strategy

    (a) Detailed plans (programme/project ownership, dates, resources, costs, expected benefits, whether/how to be evaluated) (Chapter 6)

    (b) Communication and marketing of strategy (Chapter 8) (take account of key stakeholder perspectives)

    (c) Measuring success – parameters to be used (Chapter 7)

APPENDIX B: THE ELEMENTS OF STRATEGIC HRD – A CHECKLIST

	Principles – a 'mindset of learning'		Populations needing learning
1	An integrated culture of learning is promoted as part of the organisation's value system. This culture is defined and owned by senior management, and understood by all in the company	9	Populations and communities with common types of learning need have been identified
2	Learning professionals spend a lot of their time building and supporting the overall learning culture	10	A set of learning offerings has been specifically targeted for each
3	Sharing knowledge and learning across functions and geographies is a normal expectation	11	Learning provision is vertically integrated: ■ Each 'population' receives the same core messages ■ Corporate methodologies are given to all
4	Managing on-the-job learning (through induction, coaching, managed experiences, team knowledge sharing) is a part of everyday life	12	Populations are linked to sets of business and personal competences that particularly apply to them. Progression through the organisation is through a series of assignments that enable cumulative building of such competences.
5	Everyone is able to recognise their own learning needs, define them as 'SMART' learning objectives (specific, measurable, achievable, relevant and time-related), and choose from a range of learning modes that best suit their style and the need		
6	L&D professionals are able to facilitate all modes of learning		
7	The learning strategy includes ongoing provision that maintains ■ core cultural values ■ core business competences ■ leading people through transitions		
8	The investment in learning is a key business ratio used for external and internal benchmarking		

	Processes for effective learning		Programmes in the portfolio
13	Accountabilities for learning are clear – for senior management, for line managers, for associates as individuals, for learning professionals, for L&D managers, and for suppliers	17	A manager, team or employee with a learning need has easy access to the options available to meet the need. Learning provision is horizontally integrated – from the point of view of any member of a population, it is clear where to source learning
14	There is a comprehensive and systematic language for describing levels of capability, that enables gaps to be specified and learning objectives to be set	18	The choice of offerings is made against clear parameters, which balance costs against the benefits of eg culture and values maintenance, investment in individuals, and enhanced business effectiveness. The balance between organisational, team and individual learning interventions is deliberately chosen
15	The investment in learning is driven primarily by the business through constant dialogue at sector and team level, ensuring there is always learning support for: ■ business goals and strategies ■ change initiatives A clear methodology links these business goals with defining the capabilities needed to support them	19	Learning programmes are seen as a process – including pre- and post-event activities. Several modes of learning are utilised to complete the cycle
16	Processes and tools connect different aspects of learning: ■ business planning to learning planning ■ career and succession planning reviews with personal development plans ■ career planning with transition support ■ on-the-job learning with knowledge management	20	Clear learning objectives are set, either for individual competence growth, for individual or team performance, for organisational change or for 'bottom-line' enhancement
		21	Evaluation is made against these objectives using a commonly accepted tool

INDEX